IT'S OKAY TO CRY

*Warm, Compassionate Stories
That Help You Find Hope and Healing
After the Death of a Pet*

MARIA LUZ QUINTANA

SHARI L. VELEBA

HARLEY KING

MARIPOSA PRESS

Published by:
Mariposa Press
875 Maple Street
Perrysburg, OH 43551
(800-247-6553)
E-mail: MLQKing@aol.com

Editorial Assistance provided by PeopleSpeak. Cover design by Catherine Lau Hunt. Book design and composition by Beverly Butterfield. Printed and manufactured in the United States of America on acid-free paper by Sheridan Books, Inc.

First edition: February 1998
Paperback edition: April 2000

ISBN 0-9655936-1-4

IN LOVING MEMORY OF MY SISTER,
Rosa Maria Quintana,
WHO LOVED HER DOGS, ESPECIALLY
Nimbus

Contents

How to Use This Book   ix

The Nature of Grief   xi

Lassie   1

PD, Sparkle, Bear, Mac and Daisy   12

Butch, Happy, and Spunky   20

Ramses   26

Brittney   34

Susie Marie   39

Fezziwig   49

Ginger and Hank   54

Rebel   60

Wizard   67

Schnooky   72

Cookie Marie   80

Homer and Heidi   88

Axel   94

Smoky and Snorkel   100

Felicia   104

Monty   111

Snuggle and Sandy Jo   115

Sugar   122

Lady, Sophie, Bandit, and Ingrid   127

Strawberry and Lady Bird   133

Rocky, Eugene, Pancho, Maybe and Others   137

Fair Molly MCQ   144

Nick   151

Grief Support Writing   155

Grief Journal   161

How to Use This Book to Help You Heal Your Pain and Your Grief

This book is not meant to be read from cover to cover but is designed to help a person who has lost a pet through the grieving process.

Read the book slowly—only two or three stories per sitting. Reading more than this can be overwhelming. Do not read the stories in order. Skip around.

Give yourself permission to cry as you read. Crying is healthy and helps you through the grieving process. Give yourself time to cry. Cry until you laugh. Don't be afraid of your feelings.

After you have read a story or two, write down your thoughts and feelings in the journal at the end of the book. Follow the grief writing suggestions. Writing in the journal is a powerful way to help yourself work through the grief.

If you lost a cat, read some of the cat stories first. If you lost a dog, begin with the dog stories. Don't limit yourself, though, to only cat stories or only dog stories. Read stories of different animals. The emotional experience of the person is more important than the type of animal involved. Read the stories of people who have lost professional working animals, such as Lassie, the movie star, or Axel, the police dog.

Remember that you are not alone. Others have experienced the pain that you feel and have come through it. You can learn from their experiences. Remember that the advice people share is based on their personal experience and may or may not fit you. Some of the advice will appear to be contradictory. Some people say to go out and buy a new pet immediately. Others say they will never own another pet. You must choose what is best for you.

You will find that different stories will affect you in different ways. You will not connect emotionally with every story. Some stories will have a greater impact on you than others. Identify the stories that touch you the most and reread these stories again and again because they can be a catalyst in healing your pain and grief. Each reading is a step in your journey toward self-healing.

Some stories may be too painful for you initially. Return to them later when your spirit is ready. Remember that you are in charge of your own healing. This book is only a salve to help you through the process. Proceed at the pace that is best for you.

The Nature of Grief

Maria Luz Quintana

Death is a subject that is not easily discussed because it makes us feel uncomfortable. We wish that death did not exist, but it is a part of life. As humans, most of us believe that we are in control of our lives, but when we are forced to face death, we feel weak and vulnerable. Even the most fatalistic individual will fight with tooth and nail to save a loved one from death. And when we can't change the inevitable outcome, then we may become overwhelmed by deep emotions and tears.

While taking a death and dying class in college, I decided to write a book on the subject. After doing research, I realized that very few books had been written about the grief that people experience after the death of an animal companion. I decided to write this book to give grieving pet owners a voice.

When the well-known medical doctor and psychiatrist Elisabeth Kübler-Ross wrote a book on death and dying, she interviewed over 200 patients who were dying from terminal illness. Dr. Kübler-Ross learned that the dying patients experienced five stages of grief: denial/isolation, anger, bargaining, depression, and acceptance.

We interviewed over 100 pet owners who experienced emotional reactions similar to those described in Dr. Kübler-Ross's book, *On Death and Dying,* with some key differences. We found that bereaved pet owners experienced denial, anger, guilt, bargaining, depression, and resignation during their painful ordeal. The six reactions are not progressive stages or a series of events, but instead they are emotional responses to the death of a pet. The order, frequency, and length of time the emotions are experienced will vary by individual.

Guilt was one of the most painful reactions that many pet owners experienced when they had to euthanize their pets. Even when a pet is dying from a fatal illness or has to be put to sleep because he has gotten so old that he can't control his bodily functions, the pet owner still feels guilty. Having to decide to euthanize a beloved pet creates a mental struggle in the minds and hearts of pet owners. The feeling of not knowing whether it is the right step to take can make the pet owner feel guilty.

In her book, Dr. Kübler-Ross describes the final stage as the acceptance stage. In this stage, the patient is described as "neither depressed or angry about his 'fate.'" In our interviews, we discovered that the final emotional reaction is resignation rather than acceptance because no one actually accepts the death of a loved one but rather resigns oneself to it. In resignation, the pet owner feels that she is no longer in control. There is nothing she can do that will bring back her beloved pet. The reality of death hits home. The grief becomes silent.

Throughout my youth, I experienced several pet losses. One of the most painful pet loss experiences was when one of my dogs was shot in the head. My family and I were on vacation in Mexico when this horrible incident happened. Our neighbor told us that our dog, Butch, was trying to protect our home when he was shot by a burglar. Butch managed to scare the burglar away.

When we returned from our vacation, Butch was hiding underneath our home. He was still alive with the bullet in his head. My father attempted to get him out from underneath the house, but Butch growled at him, so he decided to call the dog warden. When the warden came and captured him, Butch looked so frightened. There was blood on his head and face. When I saw his fearful eyes, tears rolled down my cheeks.

The dog warden and his assistant took Butch away and I never saw him again. It was a time of loss and sadness for my family.

Butch had been my pillow during my siestas and had been a warm shoulder when I was sad. His coat had been like a handkerchief when I cried. Losing Butch was like losing my security blanket.

For many years, I felt anger and guilt for not being with my friend when he needed me. I felt his fear and loneliness. It still bothers me that I wasn't there. I know that Butch was a dog, but he was also my amigo.

When we are children and our favorite toy or security blanket is taken away, we cry desperately. If we as adults can understand and respect the tears of a child when an inanimate object has been taken away, then we should be able to respect the tears of a bereaved pet owner who is grieving for the loss of her animal companion who has given her unconditional love.

People experienced the six emotional reactions in different ways. Some cried for a few days and some took a year or more to grieve. Here are some examples of the emotional reactions.

Denial

When a beloved animal companion is dying or has died, the pet owner finds herself in a state of shock, often overcome with feelings of numbness and disbelief. The owner is emotionally paralyzed and expresses disbelief and doubt. The daily routine that the owner and her pet shared together continues for a while after the pet dies because it is hard to believe that the animal is gone.

Kathy M. Southward was in shock when she couldn't find a heartbeat on her eight-month-old puppy, Peanut. She remembered saying, "This isn't true. This is a nightmare. I'm going to wake up and it will be over and he will be okay."

Recalling the death of her cat, Tara Cohen said, "Although I knew that Wizard was gone, I would still look for her. She used to sleep next to me, so for a while I thought she was still in bed."

Diane Welshans remembered when her dog, Peanut, a Yorkie, died in her arms. She said, "I sat down on a chair, and Peanut had another stroke, and this time I knew he wasn't coming back. He just went to sleep while I was holding him. I called to my husband, who was still in bed, and said, 'Peanut died. He's dead.' I just kept looking at Peanut, hoping he would come back, but he didn't." Later, when she took Peanut to be cremated, she kept asking the crematory workers if they were sure that he was dead.

Anger

The bereaved pet owner is filled with anguish and mortification. Most of the anger is directed toward himself or others and sometimes at the pet for dying.

Jeff Madden woke one morning to find Polly, his parrot, dying in her cage. When the vet said there was nothing he could do, Jeff's reaction was emotional: "I exploded. I screamed, hollered, and cried."

Rob Simmons, who experienced the loss of his dog, Kiya, because he accidentally ran over her, remembered, "I was mad at Kiya for lying in the driveway. And I was mad at me for being in a hurry and not checking behind the car."

Rose L. Allen, who lost her beloved basset hound, Sad Sack, said, "I would find myself angry for allowing Sack to suffer because I was too selfish to let him go."

Guilt

Whether the animal died from an accident, old age, or euthanasia, the pet owner feels a sense of guilt for the animal's death. Deep remorse is felt after a pet has been euthanized. Logically, people know that they did everything they could possibly have done for their pet, but emotionally, many still feel anguish. They feel that they could have done something more to prevent their pet from dying.

Lisa Wayne had to put her dog Mookie to sleep to protect her child, but she still felt guilt. She said, "I felt guilty with Mookie because I was the one who took her to be euthanized." Denny Rule, whose dog, Susie Marie, died in his arms, said, "I kept blaming myself. I should have taken her back into the vet's.... There is always the regret of 'If I would have done this or would have done that.'"

Bargaining

The pet owner may make promises to God for the well-being of her pet. This reaction is not experienced by every pet owner because some pets die unexpectedly.

When Darlene Czerniak's sick rabbit, Lea, was dying, she found herself bargaining with God: "I would ask God again and again to take me instead."

Deborah Prisco, whose dog, Schnooky, died of renal failure, said, "I bargained with God. I prayed that if he would make her better, I would try to be the best person in the world."

Depression

The pain of loss may become unbearable and mood swings prevalent. Bereaved pet owners find themselves crying unexpectedly at different times of the day. Any reminders of their beloved companions make them cry. They experience a loss of appetite. They are overwhelmed with sadness and will spend more time sleeping. During this time, bereaved pet owners may make drastic changes such as leaving their jobs. They have a need to grieve alone or with someone who will listen and not judge them. This is the time when few words are appreciated.

For Jeff Madden, any reminder of Polly would cause tears to appear. He said, "There were days when I would see her picture or look at her cage and I would get depressed."

Kathy Southward was overwhelmed with sadness when Peanut died: "I cried for three days, and I didn't eat for two days."

Jayne Zabrowski said, "Jack and I cried for days after Brittney died. I could not stop crying."

Resignation

Resignation is the final emotional reaction where grieving pet owners symbolically take off their boxing gloves and begin to passively accept the reality of their pets' death. They stop blaming themselves for the death of their pets. There is a sense of peace. They no longer resist the reality of the loss, but they refuse to forget their departed animal companions. The memories become less painful. They can share the happy memories with fewer tears of sorrow.

While some people are ready to share their lives with another pet, their former companions will be remembered in their hearts and stories. The relationships that they shared will be a beautiful chapter in their lives. While the pets will never be forgotten, the painful memories will be put to rest. Most people don't accept the death as much as become resigned to it. They begin to share their stories of their beloved animal companions.

Marsha Rule, whose dog, Susie Marie, died of congestive heart failure, said, "I have accepted her death because if she were alive, she wouldn't be healthy anymore. Her life would not be fulfilling."

Memories of the good times people spent with their beloved pets are cherished and shared with friends and relatives. While there still are some tears, there is also laughter whenever they remember their pets, and they are able to smile again.

Deborah Prisco said, "The pain is eased when I remember what a great life we had together."

∽

These six emotional reactions to the death of a beloved pet were not experienced in any particular order by the pet owners we interviewed nor did everyone experience all of the reactions.

I do not claim to be a doctor or a psychiatrist or an expert on death, just a human who has experienced the death of a loved one. Death has taken family members, friends, and animal companions from my life. Each loss is felt deeply, whether it's of a human being or an animal.

The relationships we share with loved ones are very important threads in the fabric of our existence. When death ends a relationship, the feeling of loss is like a puzzle that is missing a piece. Our lives have an empty space when we lose a loved one.

Bereaved pet owners should be given permission to cry without shame or embarrassment. They are not alone. Millions of others also feel the pain they feel.

Denny Rule best described the grieving process when he said, "There is not much you can do to hurry the grieving process. It has to take its course and gradually you will get over it—after a time."

Lassie

AS REMEMBERED BY

Robert W. Weatherwax Sr.

*"I grieve for the dogs before they die. I see them grow so old
they can hardly walk. I know that I will have to put the dog to sleep,
so I grieve... After the dogs die, I am relieved because
I don't have to watch them suffer anymore."*

My father, Rudd Weatherwax, trained quite a few dogs for the movie industry. When the first Lassie movie was filmed, MGM, a film production company, hired my father as an adviser and his dog Pal as a stand-in for the female collie chosen to play Lassie. The character was written as a female dog.

My father knew that the other dog couldn't perform as well as Pal, and he continued to train Pal. One day the crew shot the scene where Lassie swims back from England to Scotland to rejoin Roddy McDowell. The other dog failed to do it, so they brought in Pal. In the scene, Lassie swims the river and comes out exhausted. My father designed it so that when Pal came out of the river, he struggled, lay down, crawled, and rolled over on his side. The director liked the performance and said, "Print—this dog is now Lassie." That's how Pal became Lassie. Pal swam in and Lassie swam out.

The director also found that he liked male collies better because the males don't lose as much hair as the females. In those days it took six months to make a movie. During the winter a female collie loses her coat so badly that it changes how she looks. We couldn't have a movie where in one shot Lassie had a full coat of hair and in another shot she didn't have any hair. Although my father was very happy to have a job for Pal, he didn't realize the potential success of the movie. Lassie became the fifth highest grossing movie star at MGM during the 1940s. He grossed $268 million. He did about $30 million a year, which put him right behind Spencer Tracy for gross.

Pal, the original Lassie, and I were born one year apart to the day. Pal was born June 4, 1940, and I was born June 4, 1941, so I grew up with him. My father used me as a training prop to help train Lassie because his character had to play with little boys. I taught Lassie to kiss my cheek. I have a picture of when I was six years old and Pal was holding my hand in his mouth. My father was teaching Pal to take me to him. Lassie would gently pick me up by the arm and take me to my father.

When I travel, people come up and ask me, "What's it like to own Lassie?" Since I grew up with him, I didn't realize I was special. I thought that everyone had a dog who worked at the studios. I didn't tell anyone at school about Lassie because it was embarrassing. I was afraid the other children would say, "You don't own Lassie. We all own Lassie. You are a liar." Then I would have to prove it to them. So I never told anybody that my father owned Lassie.

My family lived isolated from our neighbors because we had forty dogs. I communicated with the dogs because I didn't have many children to play with. Since my siblings and I are almost nine years apart in age, I grew up almost as an only child. When I was a kid, my parents would find me sleeping in the kennels with some of the dogs—usually the puppies. The dogs were my family.

We didn't have a fence around our house because my father didn't have a lot of money. My father told me that when I was three years old, I once headed into the street, and Pal herded me back to keep me safe. Pal was in front of me, blocking my way, barking, and trying to move me back into the yard. My father heard him and rescued me. Collies are herding dogs by natural instinct. They like to put things in a spot and keep them there. They will take a herd of sheep and put them in a corner.

Pal was given to my father by Howard Pack, a dog trainer, because Pal chased motorcycles, and Pack couldn't break him of the habit. My father never could either. Since there were no jobs for collies at that time, my father didn't need the dog, so he shipped Pal to a man named Duke York. He told York that if he needed Pal he would come and get him. In those days my father couldn't afford to keep a dog that couldn't get a job. When the opportunity to work in the movie *Lassie Come Home* came along, my father wrote York a check and on the back wrote "Paid in Full" so that he owned the dog free and clear.

My father retired Pal after he did a television pilot with him in 1953. There have now been eight generations of Lassies. All Lassies are descendants of the original Pal—father and son all the way down. Other than Pal, none of the dogs had names other than Lassie. Lassie was the only name the dogs responded to. When the collies were puppies, we would call them "Yip Yip." As they grew, they became Laddie and then Lassie. When they retired, they became the "Old Man."

My father and I had reference names, so instead of saying Lassie Number Three or Number Four, we would use their nicknames. I was responsible for creating most of the nicknames. I called one of them "Hey-Hey." When my father and I were talking, he would ask if I remembered this Lassie and I would ask if he meant Hey-Hey. My father had one collie he called "the Baby" because he had a special affection for him.

Hey-Hey was number five. He was the last Lassie to do the Lassie television series. When Hey-Hey retired, my father went to Lassie number six. He did *The Magic of Lassie*, then he passed away. I got Lassie number seven when he was eleven months old. We did two years with Universal and the new Lassie show. Now he is retired, so I have Lassie number eight.

All the Lassies had different personalities. In general, collies are good-natured dogs, but like any individual, each had a different personality. Hey-Hey was one of my favorites because he was outgoing, loved to work, and was fun to be with.

I developed a habit of giving Hey-Hey a doughnut every morning, and he enjoyed having it because he had a sweet tooth. My father and his assistant trainer would often arrive at the set early because they wanted to rehearse a shot, but they couldn't work with Hey-Hey until I got there and gave him his doughnut. When I arrived, my father would teasingly say, "Give him the damn doughnut so we can go ahead and film this dog. I hate you and that dog because I can't work with him until you get here."

Hey-Hey was a wonderful dog. He was very easy to work with because he had plenty of energy, and we could get a complete scene out of him. I have found it easier to slow a fast dog down than to speed up a slow dog.

Hey-Hey played in the last five years of the television series, then he retired. The series ended when he was twelve, and he died when he was thirteen. I liked him because my father let me do half of the show. My father was older and didn't want to do as much of the work, so I would work with the dog in the afternoon, and my father would take the rest of the day off. Since my father was letting me do more and more of the training, Hey-Hey and I became very close.

My father loved the Baby because he was very versatile like Pal. There wasn't much the Baby couldn't do. The Baby was a slower working dog than Hey-Hey. He was a bit lazy and didn't have the fire that Hey-Hey had. The Baby, though, was very good at working with people and expressing affection like in the scenes where he had to put his head on the boy's lap then look up and kiss him. The Baby was very good with the sensitive stuff. He had these beautiful sorrowful eyes.

All actors are different. Some play more of a macho role, and some play a more sensitive role. Montgomery Clift was a more sensitive actor, and John Wayne was more rough and tough. Hey-Hey was like John Wayne, and the Baby was more like Montgomery Clift.

Collies are not the easiest dogs to train since they are bred to be sheepdogs. They have been bred to be with one person, the herder, and they have been bred to be very suspicious. In the movies, Lassie is a very gregarious, outgoing, afraid-of-nothing type of dog. We have to socialize the Lassies from a young age to make them different from what they have been bred for, so we take a little longer to train them. Only Pal and the Baby could snarl and show their teeth because it is normally not a collie trait, so they would do their own attacks.

We spend about 3,000 hours training each Lassie. We use verbal cues instead of hand signals. We direct all his moves with voice inflection. By using my voice, I don't have the dog looking at me continuously. If I used hand signals, I could not always place myself in the proper position. When I use my voice, Lassie does not have to look at me, and he responds to the actor based on my voice command. When I am dealing with a dog that does 100 tricks, I could never keep all the hand signals straight. We use voice signals 90% of the time.

For example, in the movie I made where a truck driver gets killed, I controlled how Lassie looked through my voice. I put my head down and I talked to him with a certain tone of voice, and his head dropped because he shouldn't look happy that his master was killed.

Collies are tougher to train than shepherds because I want them to like things that they normally don't like. I have to change their nature. When I train a German shepherd to pick something up, I cut the training time in half because shepherds like sticks. I can train four shepherds in the time it takes me to train one Lassie. Collies are bred not to like anything like sticks because they are a distraction from their work as herders, so I have to build that into their behavior. Collies are also very clean dogs. They don't want anything on their feet. They don't like to go through mud.

When we shoot a movie, the technicians do the lighting with a stand-in dog because I'm not going to let Lassie sit there for fifteen minutes while they experiment with the light. When the stand-in dog goes out, Lassie goes in and does the scene. It is very much the same as with human actors. The actors don't do all the work because they would be worn out.

Lassie stays in the house and has his own bedroom. Although I have fourteen other dogs, I don't keep them all in the house. I have three little ones that stay with Lassie. One is a Jack Russell terrier named Mel-Mel.

Mel-Mel and the current Lassie are about six days apart in age. Mel-Mel travels everywhere with Lassie because collies become very lonely. They like to have somebody they can communicate with. When Lassie goes to the park, he hangs out with Mel-Mel. He gets tired of being with people.

I use Mel-Mel in our current act as the comedy relief because he is the opposite of Lassie. Lassie will do fifteen minutes and Mel will do five minutes. Mel-Mel gets the laughter, and Lassie gets the oohs and ahs.

We travel about 100,000 miles a year. Lassie rides first class in an airplane. I buy a ticket for him and request the area behind the bulkhead where he has a nice large space to lie down. He does not occupy a seat because it would be too uncomfortable for him. Mel-Mel travels in a carry-on case that I strap onto a seat. As soon as we are in the air, they both go to sleep.

Lassie is brushed up to ten times a day. He gets a bath before he goes out, and he is brushed before we go into the airport. Every time he is to appear in public, he is brushed. He stays in suites in hotels like the Ritz Carlton, so he doesn't get too dirty. He travels by limousine.

Lassie brings a lot of happiness to people. I take Lassie to burn clinics for children, cancer clinics, and events sponsored by the Make a Wish Foundation for children who are terminally ill. Lassie brings them happiness and lights up their lives for a while. I can see that they haven't smiled for a long time, and Lassie gives them that moment of happiness. I feel like we are here for a reason—that we do something worthwhile.

I used to have mostly children and young mothers in the audience when I performed with Lassie. Now I probably have one-third who are children and two-thirds who are adults. The baby boomers show up today. They want to go back in time, so they come up and pat Lassie, and for a brief moment they return to their childhood and they cry.

Once a blind woman came to see Lassie. I had Lassie go over to her. He kissed her on the cheek, and she started to cry. Then my assistant, the people on the stage, and I started to cry.

Pal, the first Lassie, died of old age. I was cleaning the kennels for the other dogs when it happened. My father came out, and he was upset. Pal had lived to be eighteen. My father went through a lot when he lost Pal. He was never happy about any of the Lassies dying, but I think Pal was the toughest.

My father never watched any of the Lassie movies after he lost Pal because his theory was that he didn't like to compare them. When someone would ask him which was the best Lassie he ever worked with, he would say that it was the one he was working with at the moment.

I used to see my father praying over Pal's grave. He would stand there in silence. I wouldn't bother him because I knew it was a private moment for him. Nobody knows where the first Lassie is buried except my sister and I and a few other people, and we keep it that way.

When a Lassie had to be put to sleep, we wouldn't see my father for three or four days. He would take off because he couldn't deal with it.

We don't dwell on the passing of Lassie because there is always a new generation of people. The current Lassie is the Lassie for the children who are growing up today. We don't go into the fact that Lassies are put to sleep or say where they are buried. The children who are growing up today don't know any other Lassie but the current one.

We don't want to break the mystique of Lassie. We don't want to confuse the children. It would be like saying Santa

Claus died, and this is Santa Claus number three. There is only one Santa Claus, and there is only one Lassie.

When my dogs pass away, I have them cremated like my father did. I recently had my Shih Tzu, whom I had for twenty years, put to sleep, and he was cremated. We don't bury the dogs because we don't want any public display. We are very private, and we don't talk about our dogs' death.

Some people would come to my father crying because they had lost their pet, and he would say that the best thing to do was to get another dog to help relieve the pain. He would say, "You move on. You don't sit there dwelling on it. You move on and get another dog."

When I lost my dog from the movie *Back to the Future,* it broke me up because he was a very good dog. I was very close to him. His name was O.J. and he was a mutt—half sheepdog and half collie.

I spent a lot of time with O.J. When I spend a lot of time with my dogs, they become humanized. They are not like dogs anymore. They spend so much time with people and with the training that they become very responsive to my needs and my feelings. O.J. was so well trained that if I told him to go smell a flower, he would smell a flower. I would take him to the beach, and he would sit and look out at the waves coming in. He was like a person. He was a very good-natured dog.

O.J. was a great working dog. At the time, not very many people would use dogs in live situation comedies because they were not reliable. I had to work in silent cue, and O.J. had to be perfect because we were filming in front of a live audience. O.J. was so good at it that he opened the doors for other dogs who are now starring in sitcoms.

I was working on the new Lassie series when O.J. passed away in 1989. I had him put to sleep because he had cancer. O.J. was cremated. I don't go through any big ceremony because it is best to move on. It was good that I was working with Lassie number seven because it took my mind off the loss. It was like losing a member of the family. The dogs are like my children.

When my dogs are put to sleep, they have to be more or less stolen from me. My sister came over one night when I was out walking, and she picked up the Shih Tzu and took him to be put to sleep because she knows that I can't deal with it. My family does it for me, and they don't tell me. In the back of my mind, I know that they are going to do it, but I don't know when. They keep me out of it because I can't cope with it. When people have had as many dogs put to sleep as I have, it is difficult. The dogs are like family, and I want to give them another day and then another day. But it's not fair to them because they are in pain.

I grieve for the dogs before they die. I see them grow so old they can hardly walk. I know that I will have to put the dog to sleep, so I grieve. I put it off and put it off, so my family has to come and take the dog when I am not looking. After the dogs die, I am relieved because I don't have to watch them suffer anymore. I felt the same with my father as he grew older. I knew he was dying and the waiting was the roughest.

Death never becomes easier no matter how many dogs I lose. Fortunately, when I lose one dog, I have another one in training and that makes it a lot easier. It's best that I am busy and have something going on when it happens.

I often tell people the same thing my father did: "Go get yourself another dog. I know you don't want to do it at the moment because you feel you are betraying the other dog, but if you get yourself a cute little puppy, it helps."

My father taught me never to save any of the special toys of the dogs. When I lost my shepherd, I tried to save the little bones, but my father told me to throw them away. My father was a firm believer that a person should move on with his life. A person shouldn't dwell on the loss. This attitude was probably his savior when it came to handling the deaths of his dogs. He had to be like that. He couldn't give up and quit. I think that is how a person survives life's difficulties.

I've learned from my dogs that I have compassion. I read somewhere that the majority of people who are in prison never had a dog or any other pet. There is something about growing up with a pet that teaches you responsibility and gives you compassion. A person learns to think of individuals besides himself. I believe that it is very healthy for a child to grow up with a pet. I have seen people who don't have pets who become very cruel to animals. They are also cruel to their fellow humans because they never learned compassion. They never received the unconditional love that a pet gives.

When I was fourteen we had a dog who was going to be Lassie, but he got distemper, and in those days, we didn't know that he had to have booster shots. He stayed with me in my room above the garage, so every day I carried him up and down the stairs for him to go to the bathroom. I would feed him because he was so weak. Then we realized that he had a central nervous system disorder, and the vet said that we should put him to sleep. I had taken care of him for six months, so it wasn't easy on me. I cried when I had to carry him down for the last time. He never became Lassie. My father's heart was broken because he had put so much training into the dog and had to start all over from scratch. My father took off and left me to handle putting the dog to sleep. He left because he didn't want to deal with the pain.

When my father passed away, he left me five dogs besides Lassie. Each time I lost one of those dogs, it had a double meaning for me because not only was I losing the dog, but I was also losing a little piece of my father. Having the Lassies, though, is almost like keeping my father alive. They are all descendants of Pal, so in some way I feel like I am bringing my father along. Each new generation is linked to my father.

⌒⌒

Robert W. Weatherwax Sr. is the owner and trainer of Lassie. Since the 1940s the Weatherwax family, Rudd, Robert Sr., and Robert Jr., has raised and trained eight different Lassies as well as hundreds of other dogs for acting in television and film. Robert Weatherwax Sr. has trained over 150 dogs who have appeared in more than 150 movies and over 6,000 television episodes, including *Lassie, Married with Children, Life Goes On,* and *Simon and Simon.* Today, as a third-generation family-owned business, the Weatherwax family continues to dramatically impact the hearts and minds of millions of Americans through the character of Lassie.

PD, Sparkle, Bear, Mac, Daisy, and Others

AS REMEMBERED BY

Jack Hanna

"What I have discovered through pet loss is that I am human, that I have a heart."

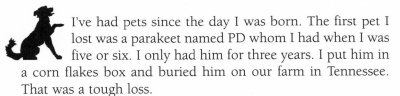 I've had pets since the day I was born. The first pet I lost was a parakeet named PD whom I had when I was five or six. I only had him for three years. I put him in a corn flakes box and buried him on our farm in Tennessee. That was a tough loss.

One Easter my parents bought me two baby goats. We named them Sparkle and Bugle. They were the first baby animals I was responsible for raising. I would bottle-feed them. I still remember their little eyes looking up at me as if to say thank you for helping them. I did not realize it at the time, but learning about the precarious nature of life helped me a great deal. More kids need to learn how to raise young animals. What is wrong with many families today is that kids are not exposed to taking care of any animals.

Shortly after we adopted the goats, my dad was pulling out of the garage and ran over Sparkle's head. My dad was devastated. He didn't know the goat was behind the car. I felt worse for my dad than I did for Sparkle. I'll never forget how my dad felt. I felt so sorry for him. My way of overcoming the pain was by telling my dad not to feel so terrible about what had happened to Sparkle.

Bugle eventually went to live on another farm, and I'm sure that he is in goat heaven by now. It has been many years since I took care of those goats, but I am amazed at how I still remember them.

My first two dogs were a couple of collies that looked like Lassie. Lance and Vandy were big, beautiful, outdoor dogs who went everywhere with me when I was little. When Lance and Vandy died, my father said that he would never have another pet, and he never did. The loss of the dogs tore him up. They are buried on our farm in Tennessee. We had a gravestone made for them. I went back fifteen years later and tried to find the gravestones, but I couldn't.

My dog Bear, a Bouvier, was very special. He looked like a bear. He had long hair because we didn't cut it. We didn't trim his ears, which grew long and floppy. Bear was a very protective dog. If somebody approached my daughters or my wife, he would become aggressive. He was would do anything for us. When we had to go out, we would leave Bear with the girls. We felt that he was their protector, their babysitter. He was a phenomenal dog.

Bear was a member of the family. He had the use of any room in the house and had anything to eat that he wanted. He would lie on the floor like a big old rug, and everybody would lie around him. Our children could do anything with him.

Bear loved to be with little animals. We would bring baby lions or baby ducks home, and he would sit with them. He slept with our cat, Willie. He was very tender and caring with the little animals, but not with other big dogs. He would tear them up, so we had to keep him inside.

We had Bear for twelve years. At the end, Bear was throwing up everything. We had him x-rayed and were told that he had cancer. We took him to Ohio State University for an operation. We were going to Montana for Christmas, so I told the surgeons to operate on Bear and if they found the cancer everywhere and it was incurable, they should let the dog go. I couldn't handle being there. When I called the veterinarian who was operating on Bear, she told me that the cancer was everywhere and that there was no way she could keep him alive. I told her to let him go to sleep while he was on the operating table.

We had Bear cremated. I still have his ashes in a container at our cabin in Montana where I'm going to bury him. We plan to have a memorial service when we bury him. Once in a while I'll be in the basement, where we have the can with his cremains, and I'll talk to Bear as if he were there.

We didn't cope with Bear's loss very well. The pain and the grief lasted several weeks. It was like losing a family member. Several months after we lost Bear, we lost my dad, and eight months later I lost my mom. So I know what it is like to lose a family member. It was a bad few months. It was the first time I dealt with death like that.

We cried for several weeks after Bear's death. I'm not saying I'm a baby, but I cried. We thought about Bear like we would a parent. I think of my parents every single day. Someone once said, "It doesn't get easier, it gets harder." Time heals, but I still think of my parents every day. We think about Bear every day and remember the fun times we shared together. We look at his pictures, which help us remember him.

I could never understand why my dad wouldn't get another collie until I lost Bear. I didn't understand until I experienced a similar loss myself. People say they are sorry and that they understand, but they don't understand unless they have been through it. There is no substitute for experience.

I found myself in shock. I couldn't throw away the dog's bone and his collar. I felt like being by myself. I wondered why I couldn't have done more. Could I have kept him alive? I became angry with myself for not discovering the cancer earlier.

I expressed my anger by going out and getting another Bear, but it didn't work. I even tried a third one, and it didn't work. I can't have new parents. I can't replace someone I love.

I bargained with God for Bear to live. I know that bargaining is not the way to do things, but I still do it. We all do it.

The sadness is overwhelming when it happens, but we have one of two choices. Either we go on, or we don't go on. I have accepted the death of Bear. I wish we had more time together. I wish I had those moments back, but that is not the way life is. Life is a gift. Every day is a gift. When we get older we understand that, but sometimes I have to remind myself when I wake up, especially if I'm feeling bad or having a bad day. Life is a gift every single day. We should look at life that way, live it that way, and hopefully, live it with our pets that way.

When I lost my parents and lost Bear, I started understanding that time was growing short, so I grieved more. I think adults grieve more than children, especially when they are older. Young children tend to bawl, but they continue to live life. They grieve, but they don't keep coming back to the grief.

Grieving for my mother and father is lasting. I think about their deaths a lot more than the loss of my pet. It is not that I don't care for the pet, but my parents raised me. I learned that I am not as strong as I thought. Death can bring us to our knees quickly, and we ask for all the help we can get to save someone whom we love.

As a zookeeper and a zoo director, coping with the loss of a zoo animal can be very difficult. At the Columbus Zoo, Mac, the gorilla was a perfect example. Mac was the clan patriarch when he died of a heart attack. He was an important granddaddy, having sired the first gorilla born in captivity. He had been caught in the wild and brought to Columbus in 1951. The keepers loved him, and he was the most fondly regarded animal in the zoo.

Dianna Frisch called me to say that she'd found Mac dead when she came in that morning. She said that Mac had died quite suddenly without suffering. I was saddened because I loved Mac. He represented both the old and the new zoo. He had been caught in Africa and lived in a cage most of his life.

After Mac's body had been transferred to Ohio State for necropsy, the keepers asked me if we could bring him back for a zoo burial. I realized that it would be nice to do for all the people who wanted to remember Mac, but I didn't want people to see this as a public relations gimmick.

At first, it was to be a quiet affair with the keepers, a "members of the immediate family" type of service. Then volunteers who had worked with Mac over the years started calling and asking to attend. The newspapers also announced the funeral and some of the public attended the ceremony.

On a beautiful weekday morning about 300 people gathered outside the zoo gates, waiting for the ceremony. The maintenance people had built a beautiful casket with "Mac" inscribed in rope on the top. They picked him up in a zoo truck, and it took eight sturdy pallbearers to lift him.

We decided to bury him next to the gorilla habitat. There were people crowded all around and piles of flowers everywhere. I remember thinking that this could be the funeral of an important person. The ceremony was informal, very touching, and very respectful.

Some people spoke first. Then I said, "We're all here today to pay respects to the first gorilla to breed successfully in captivity. Mac's contribution to the survival of the species will live on long after we're all gone. Animals are usually not buried on zoo grounds, but we felt Mac and the community deserved it because of what he had done not only for the zoo but for the gorilla species. We've learned a great deal from Mac, and that's why we're here, and that's why he'll be buried here where he spent nearly all his life."

Mac's two youngsters, Oscar and Toni, were looking on. They were very quiet, and people later said the apes knew what was going on. I don't believe that, but I know they were watching the crowd, and I know that with people being so quiet, they knew something unusual was happening.

I closed the funeral by saying, "Ashes to ashes, dust to dust.

Mac did a great job for all of us." I let the flowers stay for a few days, and then we took everything away. Today there is a plaque at the site.

I took a lot of criticism for having a funeral for Mac, but I thought it was the best decision. Having it on the grounds where he started the famous gorilla family was also important. Losing Mac was losing a fourth generation—a part of history and research. It was losing an animal that I loved. Mac was a special gorilla. I loved to sit with Mac and feed him. I had to be very careful because Mac could pull my arms off. But he was so dependent on human beings.

I felt sorry for the keepers. Observing their grief was like watching the grief of a friend who has lost a parent or a child. It is extremely hard to see the grief of someone who cares for and loves an animal, whether it is Mac, a baby duck in the children's zoo, a goat, or even a fish in the aquarium. To the zookeepers, these animals are their family. Every animal means so much to these individuals.

My advice to zookeepers who have lost animals is to remember that they did the best they could. They raised the animals the best they could. They can grieve personally, but they have to be very careful grieving in a zoo situation because they are dealing with life and death every day. They have to be very careful that the grieving doesn't effect their mental judgment, especially with very dangerous animals.

At the zoo we support each other in times like these. We are all a family. Our support is each other. We learn to cope with the grief. We do the best we can, and hopefully, there will be an animal who is pregnant and another baby will be born.

Another animal that touched me deeply like Bear was Daisy, a lion. I adopted Daisy in 1970 when she was a cub. I raised her for eight years on our farm until we had a terrible accident where she took off the arm of a three-year-old boy. I was devastated. Daisy was very close to me. While no one suggested that I put Daisy to sleep, I couldn't keep her any longer, so I gave her to the Knoxville Zoo. I later brought her to the Central Florida Zoo in Sanford, Florida, where I was the director. She lived there for the rest of her life. She passed away in 1993.

I had a special relationship with Daisy. Even after four years of not seeing her, I could call her name and she would poke her head out of the cage and come over. I would bring her to the back of cage by myself where no one could see us and I would talk to her and rub her back. It was like the old days. It was amazing how she remembered me.

I often wonder what animals are thinking. I wonder how smart they are. I don't think we have begun to understand how smart dogs, cats, and other animals are. Daisy was special. I can't say that it was like losing Bear or my parents because we had been apart for so long, but I still think about her. She taught me a lot about the exotic animal world.

Professionally and personally, I believe that if there is nothing else that can help an animal, then euthanasia is the only way. When we euthanized Bear, it was tragic, but there was nothing else left to do. Animals should not die suffering. I have seen animals in Africa suffering from starvation. They sit in the hot sun waiting to die or for poachers or other animals to kill them. That may be nature's way, but it is not a pleasant way to go.

We do everything we can for an animal, but we don't want the animal to suffer. I'm glad we have euthanasia because I don't like to watch animals suffer. It is stressful when an animal has to be euthanized at the zoo, but we accept it more today than we did twenty years ago. People more and more accept euthanasia as an alternative.

Pet loss is very difficult. I've had pets since the day I was born, and I'll probably have pets until I'm dead. The loss becomes tougher as I grow older. I think that what I have discovered through pet loss is that I am human, that I have a heart. I discovered I could get through the loss, but I was probably not as strong as I thought. Nothing can bring a person back to reality quicker than the loss of someone he loved.

∞

Jack Hanna is Director Emeritus for the Columbus Zoo. He has traveled all over the world including Alaska, Antarctica, Nepal, India, Europe, Africa, South America, the Galapagos Islands, and China. He has appeared on numerous television shows including *Good Morning America, The Late Show with David Letterman,* and *Larry King Live.* Jack is the host of the successfully syndicated *Jack Hanna's Animal Adventures* television series. He is the author with John Stravinsky of the book *Monkeys on the Interstate.* He is also the author of *Jungle Jack Hanna's Safari Adventure, Jungle Jack Hanna's Pocketful of Bugs,* and *Jack Hanna's Ultimate Guide to Pets.* Jack shares his personal stories of pet loss as well as his professional ones.

Butch, Happy, and Spunky

AS REMEMBERED BY

Debbye Turner, D.V.M.

"People need to allow themselves to go through the grieving process, and they should find someone with whom they can share their feelings."

I grew up in a family of pet lovers. Everybody loved cats and dogs. Our home was like the neighborhood humane society because we would take any strays. My mom would stop along the road and pick up animals who had been injured or abandoned, so we developed a reputation as the family who took in unwanted pets. In the spring when cats are very prolific, it was not unusual for a new cat to show up on our doorstep on a weekly basis because people knew we would keep them and take care of them.

Our pets were part of our family. When we had Christmas dinner, the animals came too. They didn't get plates like us, but they received some food and special treats. Our cats took turns climbing the Christmas tree and knocking it over. We had a constant battle to keep them from playing with the decorative balls and breaking them. We couldn't put tinsel on the bottom branches because the cats would eat it and get sick. We had to consider our animals in everything we did.

My childhood dog was Butch. My parents adopted Butch when I was a year old, so I grew up with him. Butch was my best friend. I would spend my afternoons with him. I talked to him and told him my hopes and dreams. When I was upset with my mom, I would tell him about her.

Sometimes when I was upset, I would go out on the back step and cry. Butch would come up and put his head on my knees and look at me. He would whine as if saying, It's going to be okay, and he would stay with me until I had gotten over what was bothering me. Then he would jump back and look at me as if to say, Okay, let's play. We would play with his ball or stick.

Butch was an excellent family dog. He never tried to hurt any of us or our friends. He was also a good watchdog. If any stranger or intruder looked like he was attacking us, he became very aggressive. He was a smart dog—I swear he understood English. I could say anything, and he would react as if he knew exactly what I had said.

Butch died of old age. His organ systems began to fail. He was losing his hearing and sight. He was also becoming slow and arthritic. He loved to sunbathe under a big pecan tree that we had in the backyard. He went out there one summer day and took a nap and never woke up.

Fifteen years later, I still remember him vividly. I can describe every detail of his body, his personality, and his facial expressions. Butch was part of the family, so it was like losing a family member.

Back in those days, we usually dug graves for our pets and had memorial services. Most of my childhood pets were buried in the backyard of my home that I grew up in. We would dig the hole and have a ceremony and put them in. I would pick some roses from my grandmother's garden and put them on the graves to commemorate and memorialize their lives.

Since my mother was a counselor, we would talk about death. When Butch died, my sister and I shared what Butch meant to us, and my mother explained the difference between life and death. My mother said a prayer for us that we would be able to handle the grief and would always remember him.

Years later, I would still have the impulse to go to the back door and call Butch because that's what I had done every morning of my life. It was my job to feed him. For a long time after Butch died, I didn't know what to do with myself when I woke up in the morning. My routine was broken.

Another pet that I remember vividly was our first Siamese cat. We bred and raised Siamese cats while I was growing up. Our first Siamese was named Happy because she was loving, unlike the reputation of most Siamese cats.

Happy would give me hugs and rub her nose on my cheek. I think that she thought she had hands. She was always patting my face with her paws. She looked like she had a smile. Happy's tail was always up, and her ears were always perky.

Happy didn't know that she was a cat. She was sure that she was human and maybe even superior to human beings. Instead of sticking her head down into a can of cat food, she would dip her paw in the can and nibble the food off her paw.

Happy was also very nurturing. We had another cat named Kitty. They would steal each other's kittens. Both of them had strong maternal instincts. If Kitty had a litter of kittens and Happy didn't, Happy would carry the kittens one by one to a hiding place. An hour or two later Kitty would find them and carry them back to their original spot. Eventually, they would divide up the litter. Happy would take care of one group of kittens and feed them, and Kitty would take care of the other group.

Happy lived to be fifteen years old and died of renal failure— her kidneys gave out. The last week before she died, Happy was in and out of the veterinary clinic. On the day that she died, I was spending the night at a friend's house, and my mom called the next morning. She said, "I'm sorry, sweetheart. Happy died last night."

I was devastated. I did not want to play anymore. My friends, who were twins, didn't have any pets, so they didn't understand how I felt. They kept saying, "Snap out of it and let's go play." I was frustrated by their attitude. When I arrived home, we had a memorial service and shared our grief over the loss of Happy.

I wasn't angry or shocked over the deaths of Butch and Happy. They were both old and had lived a long time. I felt sadness for the loss of two special friends.

I never felt guilt over the loss of Happy or Butch, but I did over another dog named Spunky. I still regret the way I handled the situation. I was twelve years old, and our neighbors had a big puppy who was half German shepherd and half St. Bernard. The puppy didn't know that he was big because he would sit on people's laps and put his paws on their shoulders like a baby. Our neighbors couldn't keep Spunky, so they came and asked us if we wanted him.

I begged my mom, "Oh, please! Oh, please! I promise I'll take care of him." She let me have him with the understanding that he would be my responsibility, including the feeding, the exercising and the veterinarian bills.

I had a newspaper route, so I had my own money for the first time in my life. When I received my first paycheck, I had a decision to make. Spunky had not finished having all his vaccinations, and I also wanted my own phone for my bedroom. I had to decide between Spunky's vaccinations or getting my phone. I decided to buy the phone and to have Spunky vaccinated the following month.

In that short month, Spunky developed the signs of distemper and died. And that is one of my regrets in life—Spunky didn't have to die. I had the money, and I chose the phone over the life of my dog. I felt extremely guilty because his death was preventable. He had to have been only about nine months old when he died. I was upset at myself because I had made the wrong decision. I knew it was an irresponsible and selfish decision. I accepted the responsibility for his death. I had an overwhelming sense of regret—I felt guilty.

Spunky probably didn't suffer a lot. I found him when I went out to feed him. We lived in a house that was raised off the ground. The dogs went under the house to sleep. I called Spunky, but he didn't come. I kept hearing a noise like a growl. I reached under the house and touched his paw, but he didn't respond. He was paralyzed from his neck down—the disease had affected his nervous system. I touched his head, and he snapped at me. We called the veterinarian, and he euthanized Spunky.

Dr. Jones tried to comfort me by saying that Spunky's death might have been unavoidable since he may already have been exposed, so the vaccination might not have helped. But I'm going to wonder forever whether he would have lived a long life if I had vaccinated him. I was extremely upset.

I had a terrific mom—she helped me deal with the grief and the hurt and disappointments that I had suffered in life. My mother said, "Let this be a lesson." She helped guide me through the process because it was her area of expertise. Having a family atmosphere that was understanding helped me cope. No one teased or criticized me for being sad. Anytime I wanted to talk, I could always open up and didn't have to be afraid about sharing my feelings.

Because of my mother, I have always had a balanced view and a good understanding of what happened. Though I missed the pets and was sorry they died, I was thankful to have had them in the first place. Even though I hated that Butch died, I am glad that I had those fourteen years with him. The memories will never leave.

My mother died unexpectedly, and I inherited Blessed, one of her cats. There have been times when I have cried because I miss my mom, and Blessed will try to comfort me. She will come up and start rubbing on my head and meowing. She does this only when I'm crying. My mother's death has put everything else in perspective.

I am a sensitive person. For example, when a horse gets killed in a movie, I am emotionally distressed. I loved the movie *The Lion King,* but I was distraught because the father lion died. I had to leave the theatre and pull myself together.

As a veterinarian and an animal lover, euthanasia is still difficult for me to deal with. I have assisted with the process, but I have never done it by myself. I understand that there are specific situations where euthanasia is called for and is the humane action to take, but on a personal level, I value the lives of animals very highly. I don't believe that any person who has a heart and compassion for the life of an animal is ever truly comfortable with euthanasia. I volunteered once for a veterinarian who had been practicing for almost thirty years, and he was still not used to it.

The last time I had to sit in and observe an animal being euthanized, I had to leave the room because I knew the history of the animal. I knew the animal had been in the family for fifteen years and the pet had fought diabetes for three or four years. I knew the people loved their pet, and it was tough for them to lose him. I could feel their pain.

I hate to hear people say, "Oh, why don't you get over it—it was just a dog. Why don't you get another dog?" You can't replace a pet. You can get another pet, but he'll never be the one you lost. That's not the way to grieve. You have to grieve first, and then get another pet if you want one. Don't discount the relationship with the pet who died. People need to allow themselves to go through the grieving process, and they should find someone with whom they can share their feelings.

Dr. Debbye Turner is the 1990 Miss America as well as a veterinarian. Dr. Turner became a veterinarian because of her love of both animals and science. The family veterinarian served as her role model while she was growing up in Jonesboro, Arkansas. Dr. Turner currently does public relations and public education in the veterinarian field and is a spokesperson for Ralston Purina. She hosts a pet care show on PBS called *The Gentle Doctor.* She is also a motivational speaker, delivering about 200 speeches a year. She shares her feelings about the death of her dogs, Butch and Spunky, as well as her cat, Happy.

Ramses

AS REMEMBERED BY

Patricia A. Nelson

"I believe that our loved ones never die as long as the memories are there and people keep sharing their stories."

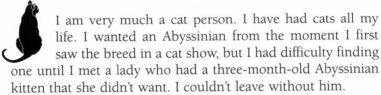 I am very much a cat person. I have had cats all my life. I wanted an Abyssinian from the moment I first saw the breed in a cat show, but I had difficulty finding one until I met a lady who had a three-month-old Abyssinian kitten that she didn't want. I couldn't leave without him.

The Abyssinian cat is thought to be the original feline of Egypt. Since I had been to Egypt, I decided to name the kitten after a famous Egyptian pharaoh, either King Tut or Ramses. He seemed more like a Ramses, so I called him Ramses.

When I adopted Ramses, I had three other cats and a Great Dane. I was very close to my other pets, but Ramses and I immediately formed a wonderful bond.

Abyssinians tend to be one-person animals, and they usually are not very friendly with other cats. In the beginning my other cats were afraid of him. I found it funny because Ramey thought they were his friends.

Oscar, my Great Dane, was very lovable. When Oscar would lie down, Ramses would come up, sniff him, and pounce on his tail. Oscar would wake up, and Ramses would jump up to the ceiling. Ramses was not afraid of Oscar. He loved to play with Oscar's big unclipped ears.

Ramses was my baby, and I treated him as a little baby. I carried him around in a blanket, so naturally, he always wanted to be carried. If I was in the bathroom, he would hop up on the sink and would try to climb into my arms. He wanted to sit on my shoulder and walk around the house with me. I spoiled him.

Ramses was not a shy cat. When we had company, he was the host. If somebody came to the front door, he would greet them. Most of my cats hid under the couch, but not Ramses. He assumed that everybody liked cats. He was very outgoing, and even people who didn't like cats were fascinated by his charm.

Ramses was also very curious, which is another Abyssinian characteristic. He would follow me around the house. My Himalayan and Persian cats lay around, but Ramey was always with me. He would observe everything that I did from washing the dishes to changing the litter box.

Sometimes Ramey put my shoelace or a string from one of his toys in his mouth. He would drop the string in front of me, make a special chirping sound, and then look at me in expectation. I would tell him thank you. He would purr and rub up against me. Then I would reward him for bringing me the object.

Sometimes he would bring me spiders. He would jump on my bed with the spider in his mouth. I would say, "No, Ramses," and he would let it go. Sometimes the spider would still be alive, and Ramey and the other cats would chase the spider around my bed.

I attached a couple of fake spiders to a fishing pole and would swing the fake spiders in the air, and Ramey would do double loops and backflips. He would go crazy chasing the fake spiders.

Unfortunately, Abyssinians have many physical problems. As Ramey was growing up, he had a lot of problems with his gums. I brushed his teeth with a little toothbrush.

I noticed one day that Ramses was drinking more water than normal, so I took him to the vet, who diagnosed him with kidney disease. The prognosis was bad: Ramses only had four to six months to live. I told the vet to work with me because I wanted to keep Ramey alive and didn't want him to suffer. I wanted him to have a good quality life until the end.

The vet told me that I should give Ramey fluids, which would flush out the impurities from his system. His kidneys were not functioning well, and the fluids would help his condition. I also had to put him on a low protein diet with vitamins. The vet gave me recipes for special food.

For nineteen months I gave Ramey fluids with an IV bag every two to three days. I would put Ramey on my lap and stick the needle in the back of his neck. He didn't even feel the needle. Ramey would stay on my lap and quietly purr, and I would scratch him under the chin. We'd sit in my bedroom with the door shut to keep the other cats out. It was our time together. If I had not had a close relationship with Ramey, I don't think I would have been able to run the IV.

When I took Ramses to the clinic, the vet warned me about the reality of his condition. I think that he was preparing me for the inevitable. Ramey was healthy except for his kidneys. All his lab work was normal. He had lost weight, but he gained it back. Ramey was active and played with the other cats.

In January, Ramey stopped eating. I tried to feed him, but he wouldn't eat. The day before I took him to the vet for the last time, I carried him around wrapped in a blanket so he could see my two other cats. I also took him outside because he loved to see the birds.

I took Ramey to the vet because he was going to make one last effort to help Ramey. My friend, Kathy, and I were allowed in the intensive care unit (ICU) area to be with him for a while. The next day the vet called and told me that Ramey was in complete kidney failure.

When my boss found out that Ramey had to be put to sleep, she pulled Kathy out of a meeting and told her to meet me at the vet's. When I arrived at the vet's office, the staff had everything set up. They set aside one of their examining rooms and brought in water and a box of tissues for me. Then they brought Ramey into the room and explained the process. I had told them before that I wanted to be with him. Some people can do it and some can't. I had been there for my other pets, so I wanted to be there for Ramey.

The vet told me I could spend as much time as I wanted with Ramey. When I was ready, Ramey would be given a sedative to relax him. Kathy and I were with Ramey for about four hours, petting him, talking to him, showing him his toys. He purred and seemed to be at peace and contented to be with us. I kept asking myself and the vet if there was anyway we could save him, even though I knew there was nothing anybody could do.

The decision to put Ramey to sleep was very difficult for me to make, but I knew that it was for the best because his health had gradually gone downhill. I had always been afraid that when he became very sick, I wouldn't be able to let go of him. But as difficult as it was, I had no question in my mind because he was very uncomfortable. I reminded Ramey that I had always told him to let me know when he was ready, and I knew he was doing that now. I loved Ramey, so I knew I had to let him go. Kathy and I walked away in tears.

Kathy was supportive throughout his illness and death. She had been close to Ramey too. She would stay with my cats if I went out of town. Kathy was very sensitive through it all. She was experiencing the grief as much as I was.

When we left the vet's office, Kathy asked me what I wanted to do. I told her that I needed to go somewhere and not think about the situation for a few minutes. We went to get something to eat, then she took me home and went back to work. I stayed home for the rest of the day. My boss gave me a day off after Ramey died.

I feel that I experienced all the stages of grieving, especially denial, anger, and depression. I think that if people don't let themselves go through the grieving process, then dealing with their loss will be tougher. I was very upset when Ramey was first diagnosed with kidney disease. When he passed the six-month mark, I began thinking that he wasn't sick and that he wasn't going to die.

My vet kept telling me that Ramey was very sick, but I would say that we were going to get through this. I would point out how well he was responding to the fluids. I kept fixing the special food for him and giving him his IV. When he wouldn't eat anything, I tried to force-feed him. I kept thinking that maybe his gums were bothering him, so I would clean his teeth more often. I was in complete denial.

I should have been preparing myself for his death, but I didn't because I was hoping for a miracle. If I hadn't had hope, I don't think he would have lasted as long as he did. I kept taking care of him because I loved him.

I went through shock when I finally had to put him to sleep because I don't remember the next two days. I was numb.

I became very angry without any rational reason. I was upset because nobody had figured out how to do kidney transplants on animals. I found out later that such transplants can be done, but they are very expensive and are still in the experimental stage. The anger went on for about a week, and then on the weekend I broke down. I couldn't stop crying and went into a depression. I had an aching feeling because I missed Ramey.

For the first couple of months, the loss was extremely intense. I didn't want to go home because Ramey wasn't waiting for me at the door. Everything I had done for Ramey was like a shadow following me. What did help me go home was that I felt I needed to be with the other cats.

The memories of our time together were hard to handle. I was depressed during the holidays because I would remember Ramey playing with the Christmas decorations. I would cry whenever something reminded me of him. It was very tough to go to the vet's office. I became stressed when I had to take my other cats for routine checkups. I became depressed and didn't want to be with anybody. For three months I withdrew from everybody except my cats. I would talk to my other cats about Ramey.

For about a week after Ramey died, Tiffany and Alexandria, my other cats wouldn't eat. They both comforted me when I was crying. Tiffany walked around crying and looking for Ramey. Alexandria walked around the heat registers where Ramey slept and smelled the registers. Tiffany and Alexandria liked playing with Ramey since they were very close in age. Tiffany and Alexandria were seven, and Ramey was not quite nine years old when he died.

When I went back to work, some of my coworkers didn't know about Ramey's death, and I didn't feel the need to share that my cat had died because some people don't understand. I would respond that I had lost a very close friend. Ramey was my best friend who was always there for me.

My boss and some people at work clued other people in so they wouldn't ask me too much. Most of my coworkers said something positive to me or kept quiet. Kathy would come over, and we would talk. I liked being around her because she had been there when Ramey died.

Kathy, my dad, my boss, the vet, and my other friends were incredible throughout my painful ordeal. My vet sent me a card that was signed by the technicians and the other vets. Each of them wrote something about my relationship with Ramey or something about him. He had been going to the vet for a long time, and most of them knew him. I received flowers from some of my coworkers. Even a month after his death, I received calls, cards, and voice mail messages from my coworkers. They seemed to understand that the loss of Ramey was like the loss of a family member to me.

My father and friends were wonderful because they allowed me to grieve. I didn't feel bad about expressing my grief. I enjoyed talking about Ramey to people. People think that when a person loses someone, they shouldn't talk about it because the individual who is grieving will feel uncomfortable. But what I enjoyed the most was talking to people who knew Ramses. I felt that talking about Ramey kept him alive. Talking about Ramey and being able to remember the things that he did were very therapeutic.

When I first found out that Ramey was ill, I took him to a photo studio, and the photographer took pictures of him both alone and with me. When I called the photo studio and told them that Ramey had died, the staff made a collage of the different poses of Ramey. I had the studio blow up one of the pictures that captured Ramey perfectly.

I started a feline family album after Ramey died. I put the beautiful cards and the two poems that I received in the album. I also put in pictures of Ramey and the flowers that people sent, as well as pieces that I had written about Ramey.

I have had all my cats and my dog cremated, and I have them in individual urns. I decided to have my animals cremated because if I move, I can take them with me. I had Ramey's urn professionally done by an artist. She painted the urn to look like him, and it is beautiful. I kept his fake spider and a little shoestring that he gave me.

Funerals are more for the living than the dead. The process of getting the cremains, ordering the urn, and having something engraved is a rite of passage. When it came to the funeral arrangements, I went through the same process with my animals that I did when my mother died. The rite of passage is a very significant event for our love ones and for us.

I lost my mother before I lost Ramses. Her death was devastating. Through my grief over her, I learned that there was initially an intense grieving process, and then the loss was slowly incorporated into my life. I also learned that it was very important for me to have mementos of my mom as well as her pictures.

From my losses I learned how to deal with people when they experience the loss of a loved one, whether that loved one is a human or a pet. I learned to be more sensitive and to understand what other people's needs are when they are mourning. It is very important to allow them to talk.

I knew a woman at work who lost her dog. She felt she didn't have permission to grieve. She hadn't even told anybody about her dog. When I found out about her loss, I gave her permission to grieve. She was trying not to cry because she was embarrassed, but she finally shared her feelings. I gave her a card and some flowers.

A couple of weeks later, she told me that she had been trying to write me a thank-you letter, but she couldn't do it. I told her to continue going through her grief and that she would write the card when she was ready. A month later I received the card. People need to understand that they can't force the grieving process.

I advise people to keep a journal. In my journal, I wrote about Ramey during his last three months and after he died. The writing process helped me to express my anger during Ramey's illness. I had him for a long time after his initial diagnosis, so I was able to look at the glass as half full and not half empty. I knew ahead of time about his illness, which allowed me to spend more time with him. I felt very fortunate that I had nineteen months with Ramey before he died.

The reality of Ramey's death hit home when his cremains came back. When Ramses was first gone, I had nothing tangible, but when I received the cremains, his death became real. I broke down. I remember carrying his cremains out of the vet's office. I was holding the ashes like they were him. The ashes were the only part of Ramses that I had.

I took about a year to accept his death. Like any other pain that I have experienced in life, I had to go through it because I couldn't avoid it. Slowly, the loss became less painful. I began remembering more of the good memories than the painful loss. I felt very lucky that I had his pictures and his belongings to remember him by.

I will always love Ramey because he was very special. I believe that our loved ones never die as long as the memories are there and people keep sharing their stories.

Brittney

AS REMEMBERED BY

Jayne Zabrowski

"I cried for days. . . . I could not stop crying."

We lost Brittney, our beautiful golden retriever, in November of 1993. Brittney was such a wonderful dog. We adopted her a few months before my husband, Jack, and I were married. We never had children, so she was our family. She was with us for almost twelve years.

Before Christmas 1981, a friend of mine who owned a dog kennel called and said that the kennel had a nice-looking dog and asked if I would be interested. I replied that at this stage of my life, I didn't know if I had time for a dog.

On Christmas Eve, I told Jack that it couldn't hurt to look at the dog, so we went. The dog was so afraid that she had to be carried out of the kennel. My first reaction was that I couldn't handle this dog.

On New Year's Eve, my friend called again and said that the dog was going to be put down the next day. I had been thinking about her all week, so I decided to take her.

When my friend carried Brittney out to me, the dog leaned over and put her head on my shoulder. I wanted to give her a good home. I could not leave without her.

Brittney had been abused and was afraid of many things, including water. I think someone must have thrown her in a lake. She was also afraid of men. Whenever Jack would come over, Brittney would hide underneath a table.

I could tell that she had never been in a house. Every night she urinated on my kitchen floor. She wouldn't go near other people. After a month, I told Jack that Brittney was going to be more than I could handle. She had been abused too badly, and I didn't think I could take care of her anymore. That night she didn't urinate on the floor, so I decided to wait and see for a while. Brittney never went to the bathroom on the floor again. From that point forward, our relationship flourished.

I took Brittney to dog training classes. She was afraid of all the other dogs. I had to carry this fifty-pound dog into the building, with everybody giggling and laughing. Six weeks later, we graduated with a first-place trophy.

We never had to tie her up. We lived on the outskirts of the city, and she would just lie on the front porch or stay in our yard all day. She never had to be kenneled, chained, or leashed. People were always amazed at that. They would drive by our house and ask how we trained our dog to stay in the yard. I would tell them that I never did—Brittney knew that it was her home.

When I took Brittney to my parent's house, they never had to tie her up, even though they lived by a busy highway. Brittney was always good that way.

Whenever we went on vacation, we took Brittney. If we wanted to play golf or go shopping, we would leave her at our cottage without tying her up. She would stay there and wait for us. I think that if we had been killed or had never returned, no one would have been able to get her to move from the last location where she saw us. She adored us, and the feeling was mutual.

Brittney was a woman's dog, so she was very attached to me. I adopted her when I was single, and she was there when Jack and I were married. Brittney was with us through the good times and the bad times.

Brittney was intelligent and good with children. My friend who has triplets said, "If it hadn't been for Brittney, my kids would still be afraid of dogs." Her children's fear of dogs diminished after they met Brittney because she was very gentle with them.

The last few years of her life, Brittney had arthritis. She was on steroids, and I knew that someday I would have to make the decision to put her to sleep. I talked with the vet numerous times about what the end would be like. I wanted him to come to our home when the time came to put Brittney to sleep so I could lie on the floor with her and hold her in my arms until she died peacefully. I didn't want to take her to the clinic to be put to sleep. The vet agreed to come to my home.

The end was not like I had imagined it to be. I always thought we would know in advance and would have time to say our goodbyes.

On Thanksgiving, Brittney vomited during the night. I could tell that she was upset and wanted to spend the night outside, but she didn't. The next day I knew that she didn't feel well, so I called the vet. He said that maybe she ate something that didn't agree with her, so he recommended some Pepto-Bismol.

On Saturday morning she was still tired. She took the Pepto-Bismol but refused food, water, and Pedialyte. Later in the day she barked to indicate that she wanted to go outside. We moved her doghouse onto the deck just inches from the patio door so we could watch her. Before she went outside, she drank Pedialyte for me. I had been trying to get her to drink for two days, so I was elated when she did. I know now that it was her final act of trying to please me: Okay, if you want me to drink this so bad, I will.

We put her in the doghouse, and she curled up to go to sleep while still being able to see us in the house. I assumed that if she drank and had the strength to go outside on a cool November day, she must be getting better.

When I went to check on her, she was gone—peacefully, no mess, eyes shut like she was sleeping, but alone. Her dying alone tore my heart apart and still does, but it was how she wanted it. I think she knew that I could never have stood the pain of holding her and watching her take her last breath. She accepted her death calmly, and I would not have.

Jack and I cried for days after Brittney died. I could not stop crying. She died on Saturday night and was buried on a cold November Sunday morning. The sun came out while my husband was digging her grave. When he was done digging, we each said our goodbyes to Brittney.

We buried everything of hers with her: collars, toys, blankets, beds, and dishes. Brittney had a little stuffed teddy bear that she liked to carry around. She also had a heart-shaped bowl. We put food in it and buried it with her. We took the straw out of her doghouse and put the house up in the garage rafters. We could not handle any reminders.

Her grave overlooked our backyard and the river that wound through it. Deer ate corn nearby, and bunnies ran and played over her grave.

Every morning I would get up, look out the dining room window, and cry because I missed her. I would hear her feet clicking on the hardwood floor, or I'd hear her bark. I couldn't believe that she wasn't there. I would come home and expect her to be there.

I was angry at myself because I let her go outside and I wasn't there when she died. I wanted to be with her when she died. I kept saying, "She died all alone."

I don't think that I withdrew from my family and friends, but my husband and I withdrew from each other for a while. It was a very stressful time.

The worse thing that people can tell you is "Get another dog right away and you'll feel better."

Fortunately, I had friends who understood and even sent flowers. My sister sent three red roses in Brittney's memory. I put the roses on her grave, which was visible from our windows. A few days later I looked out the window at the spot on the deck where she died, and I saw a single rose petal with a piece of straw lying gently over it. I called my husband to see it. I couldn't believe it, so I took a picture. When I came home for lunch, I looked and everything was gone—no rose petal and no straw. I walked out to her grave, and the roses were frozen in perfect form, undisturbed, without a single petal missing.

I strongly believe that Brittney's spirit laid the rose petal and the straw for us to see. She was telling us that everything was going to be okay and that it was time for us to stop crying. She loved us too much to want us to be sad any longer.

Susie Marie

AS REMEMBERED BY

Denny and Marsha Rule

"Time will be the greatest factor in healing. On the first day you think about the grief all day long. . . . Every day that goes by is a little bit less painful. There is not much you can do to hurry the grieving process."

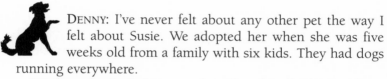

DENNY: I've never felt about any other pet the way I felt about Susie. We adopted her when she was five weeks old from a family with six kids. They had dogs running everywhere.

We brought Susie home and made a box for her, and my stepdaughter wrote "Susie Marie Campbell" on it. I thought, Gee, our name is Rule; shouldn't her name be Rule? But that's part of being a household made up of two different families.

I think she made a big adjustment possible for all us. Susie was like the common denominator for everybody. I feel that kids need a dog they can curl up with in bed when they don't feel good or when they are going through some problem. I think it was healthy for all of us.

Susie was so small that she'd trip over the garden hose in the backyard. She was a wee little bit of a thing.

MARSHA: Susie learned early that we were her protectors and that she could come running to us for protection. Two scary things happened to her when she was little. One day we were walking around the backyard when suddenly Susie came crying to us. There was a small branch in her rectum. We were afraid of hurting her, but we knew that we had to do something, so we carefully removed the branch. About a week later we were out in the backyard and she came running over to us, crying. We looked at her butt, but there was nothing there. We picked her up saw a big bug on her belly that had bitten into her skin, so Denny took it off. We became her protectors.

I trained Susie when she was little to go potty. Every few hours, I'd take her outside whether she had to go or not. I'd take Susie out after she woke up and after she ate or drank. She learned to go to the back door when she had to go potty, and I never had trouble with her unless she was sick.

Susie didn't like to go to the bathroom if it was raining and had this prance-like walk that expressed, I've got to go. She would go to the back door, and when we opened the door, she would see the rain and back up as if saying, I'll wait. I'll wait.

DENNY: When it snowed, I had to shovel a spot off so she would have an area to go potty. She never went beyond the area that was shoveled because her legs were so short.

When she was a little pup, people would pick her up and she would pee on them. She was so excited that she couldn't control her bladder. It was the very best welcome she could give.

At night Susie would put her paw on me and lick my hair to wake me up to take her to the bathroom—never Marsha. It was always me who had to do it. I was definitely the head of the pack. If you don't train dogs to know who the pack leader is, then they begin to think they are. Then you have an unruly dog. Susie knew her place in the hierarchy.

She was so humanized that when we would walk down the street and the neighbor's Beagles would bark at us, she would not even look in their direction. She had no interest in other dogs. She would walk with us without being on a leash.

I prefer dachshunds because they are not the kind of dogs that run around making noise; they are more sensible. Susie and I would sit together quietly and look at the Christmas tree, and I'd talk to her about the tree and about Christmas and what a good girl she was. She loved to be told that she was a good girl. Susie was more like a person to me.

MARSHA: But like a child, Susie loved getting into the Christmas tree. She would take the cellophane-wrapped candy canes off the tree and eat the candy. When we would come home, there would be cellophane on the floor but nothing else. One year I made cinnamon ornaments with apple sauce and glue. She got one of those off the tree and ate it.

Another time, we put up a four-foot tree with little candy canes. When we came home, the tree had been knocked off the table and Susie was shaking. She probably became scared when she heard our car.

DENNY: She knew when she was in trouble. She would sit behind a chair with her head down as if to say, I shouldn't have done it, but I couldn't resist.

MARSHA: Susie loved to go camping. When we'd load up the minivan and pack up the camper, Susie would get excited and jump into the van. And we couldn't get her out—not even by offering her candy.

DENNY: We wouldn't put her on a leash at the campsite. All the other dogs would have to be tied, but Susie wouldn't think about going anywhere else. She was part of our pack. The campsite was like home to Susie.

MARSHA: When we came home from camping, I'd put all the dirty clothes on the floor to start washing. Susie would be so worn out from the excitement that she'd lie on the dirty clothes and sleep for twelve hours.

DENNY: Susie could feel hurt, joy, and excitement. Sometimes I'd get on the floor and put my hands over my head and pretend I was crying, and she'd come up and try to comfort me. She'd slip her head underneath my arm and lie beside me.

MARSHA: One time I was very sick and was home alone. I had vertigo. I woke up in the middle of the night and tried to climb out of bed, but I couldn't because it felt like the whole room was spinning. I had to feel for the phone to call Denny at work. I couldn't open my eyes because it made me nauseated. Susie could sense that I wasn't feeling well. She came to me and licked me and tried to help.

Susie became sick the night before Shannon, our daughter, went into labor. She started shaking and wouldn't eat. She wouldn't go out of the house, even to go to the bathroom. She lay on the blanket behind the recliner chair and would not move. We tried to coax her out with food, but she wouldn't come out. She just shook. We wondered what was the matter with her, so we called the vet but got no answer.

When morning came, she was still shaking. Shannon was scheduled to have a C-section that day, but unbeknown to us, she was already in labor. When Susie saw us taking Shannon to the hospital, she ran to the door wagging her tail, then everything was fine with her. It was as if she knew that Shannon was in labor, so Susie was in labor too. As soon as Susie knew we were doing something for Shannon, she was fine.

DENNY: We bred Susie with black dachshunds so she would have an equal number of black and brown puppies. She didn't like a couple of the male dogs that we brought and wouldn't have anything to do with them. Then we heard that it is always best to take the female to the male's place because that's his area, and she is subject to his authority. If you bring the male to her house, she is going to think, Hey, buddy, this is my house.

MARSHA: When Susie was pregnant the first time, she could not even get her legs over the doorsill. We had to lift up her back to get her over. She had two litters: six puppies in the first one and seven in the second. With her first pregnancy, she had to have a Cesarean section because it took so long to deliver. We took her to a vet who gave her a shot to make the contractions stronger, but she quit pushing. Susie was afraid.

DENNY: I delivered the second bunch of puppies, which was exciting. Susie had them all naturally that time.

MARSHA: We didn't keep any of the puppies because we thought that one was enough. Since Susie was so devoted to us, I don't think she would have wanted to share us.

Denny was more emotionally attached to Susie than I was. I cried when she died, but he cried for weeks. I had other things to keep me preoccupied, so I didn't have time to think about Susie. We had Shannon's new baby in the house.

DENNY: I think it's taking me longer to get over it because I was there when Susie died. I felt so helpless. The emotion I felt hearing that long last breath and knowing it was over has been overwhelming.

Susie had been bitten by something. There were two little marks on one of her hips. The area got infected and swelled up, and when I touched it, she cried out. The mistake I made was to let it go, but I thought she would get over it. A scab formed and fell off, and her hair grew back. Then Susie became short of breath. She didn't want to go on walks anymore. She would lie on the couch with her head up on the arm to make it easier for her to breathe.

I took her to the vet, and he couldn't find anything wrong, but the symptoms persisted. Susie didn't even want to walk to the end of the driveway. I took her back to the vet, and he took an x-ray. He said that she had congestive heart failure and her lungs were filling with fluid. He gave me some pills to give her at home.

When I told him about the infection, he said that it probably settled in the valves of her heart and was causing the heart failure. He said that eventually Susie would die.

I lifted her into the car because she was too weak to jump in. I kept blaming myself. I should have taken her back into the vet's, but he had an emergency case to take care of—a dog who had been hit by a car.

I put Susie in the front seat of the Volkswagen and turned the air conditioning on so the cool air would blow on her face. Susie kept looking at me all the time I was driving.

Susie put her paws on my leg. I knew she liked to sit on my tummy—my barrel. I said it was going to be okay, but I knew it wasn't. Still driving, I put her up on my chest; she lay on my shoulder, took one last big breath, and was gone.

It was raining so hard that the wipers couldn't keep the water off the windshield. I was in second gear and couldn't shift because I was steering with one hand and holding her with the other. I drove for two miles in second gear until I reached our house. The horn didn't work on the car, so I couldn't get Marsha to come out. I laid Susie down gently on the car seat and went into the house.

I told Marsha that Susie was a lot sicker than we thought. She asked, "Susie's gone, isn't she?" And I said, "Yeah."

It was difficult to bring her into the house. Marsha held Susie's body, which we wrapped in a towel, for an hour.

I felt bad that I had been alone with her, but I felt that I gave her a little peace. I believe that she felt better because she could lay her head on my shoulder, and I told her it was going to be okay. I guess that's what I would want—I would want somebody to tell me that it's okay.

I will always feel regret: If I just would have done this or would have done that. Many remorseful emotions piled up. The hardest part was putting her in a cardboard box. I don't know why, but I yelled out, "Susie doesn't like it in the box."

We put Susie's body out in the garage because we couldn't find the right box. We took more than a day to find a box because we weren't satisfied with what we saw. We didn't want a box that would collapse, so we kept going to different stores.

MARSHA: We called several pet cemeteries. They wanted us to pay a certain amount right then as well as pay a fee each year for upkeep. The box to put her in was extra. We decided Susie would be happier at home because this is what she remembers.

We also decided not to buy a box from a cemetery because it cost a hundred dollars. We thought that if we looked long enough, we might be able to find something that was suitable and would be watertight. We eventually bought a Rubbermaid container that seemed to be the right size to place Susie and her special things inside comfortably.

We put her toys and some other items in the box because they were a part of her. Any reminders of her were hurtful to me. I wanted to close her death out of my mind if I could. I didn't want to come upon her toys later because they would bring up sad memories. Since she loved the toys and always played with them, we couldn't think of a better place for them than with her.

DENNY: The toys were worn out, especially the squeaky ones that she sunk her teeth into. She was never satisfied until she ruined the squeaker.

MARSHA: She also liked to lie down on Denny's coat, so we put that in the box with her. In nine years she had chewed up a lot of blankets, but we still had a pink blanket that she lay on, so we put it in the box.

DENNY: We buried her about three days after she died. I have a bad back, so I couldn't dig the hole. We called somebody from the tree nursery to dig a hole for us. I thought the guy was going to bring a backhoe and make a couple of swipes, but he came over with a shovel. I gave him forty dollars to dig a deep hole.

The grave digger and I carried Susie over and put her down in the hole. Marsha and I stood there with our arms around each other talking about Susie and praying. The grave digger stood behind us with his hands crossed. He was quiet and re-spectful.

I don't truly believe that animals have souls, but I like to think they do anyway. We said a little prayer asking for Susie to be with us in the next world if that was possible.

MARSHA: We called up everybody we knew, as if a family member had passed away, to let them know that Susie was gone. We were scheduled to host a Baha'i Fireside meeting on the day that she passed away, but we canceled it because we were too emotionally stressed.

DENNY: I cried in front of people at work, which was embar-rassing. A few people knew how much the dog meant to me because I would show them pictures of her. She had a little toy alligator that she thought was her baby. She guarded it fiercely. At work, people would ask jokingly, "How's Susie and her alli-gator?"

MARSHA: We received three sympathy cards from people who did understand how we felt when she passed away.

DENNY: I think the cards were from people who had dogs that had died, and they once felt the same way we did. They knew the kind of feelings that we were experiencing. They were aware of our grief.

MARSHA: The people who have pets were understanding and sympathetic. Others were indifferent about it.

DENNY: I'd tell some people about Susie, and they'd say, "I never liked dogs." Those were the first words out of their mouths. They had no interest at all. I learned to accept that.

Some people would tell us to go out and get another pet. I felt that was very cold. Would you tell a mother and father who had lost their infant child to have another baby right away? I don't think these people truly understand the nature of love. You can't replace a loved one.

MARSHA: We have vacillated about having another dog. Our lifestyle has changed a lot. We are gone so many hours during the day that the thought of having a puppy seems too much. He would be by himself for hours. We would have to house-break him and keep him from chewing on things.

DENNY: I feel that I can't have another dog. If dogs lived as long as people, it might be okay, but I can't go through losing another. It's too hurtful. Having Susie was joyful, but the pain of losing her was too great.

MARSHA: I have accepted her death because if she were alive, she wouldn't be healthy anymore. She would be taking medicine all the time, and she probably would have bladder incontinence. Her life would not be fulfilling.

DENNY: I learned something about our marriage—it's better to go through something like this with someone special than to go through it alone. Marsha was the special person to be with after Susie died—we've shared a lot of joys, and this was the biggest grief that we've ever shared. And it was good to have Marsha there.

MARSHA: The pain of it will go away. The memory will stay forever. It's like losing a family member.

DENNY: Time will be the greatest factor in healing. On the first day you think about the grief all day long. The next day, you think about it almost all day long. Every day that goes by is a little bit less painful. There is not much you can do to hurry the grieving process. It has to take its course, and gradually you will get over it—after a time. For the most part, life will go on.

MARSHA: I can still remember the hour that my mother passed away like it happened yesterday. I heard my mother's last breath. I can remember waking up and thinking that I heard it again. It's a eerie feeling. It's been twenty-two years since my mother died and thirteen years since my father died. The grief that you feel when a loved one dies goes away after a while because with time, the pain becomes less and less. You think about the person, but not every day. But when you do think about your loved one, you may pause a moment to say a prayer or to reflect on a memory, and most of the memories are good.

DENNY: A week after Susie died, a little two-year-old boy fell into a river when it was high and drowned. I felt like calling his parents and telling them that I knew what they were going through. Then I realized that I couldn't do that because they would never understand. Susie was just a dog, and the boy was their child, but we knew and understood the terrible hurt and pain they were going through.

I've never had a child of my own, but Susie was like my child. She was a big loss. Even though it is painful to talk about her, it makes us remember the love we had for her.

Fezziwig

AS REMEMBERED BY

Karen Herschleb

*"No matter how much the loss hurts, the love the
pets give me is worth more than the pain."*

My children found two stray cats and asked if they could keep them. I told them they could. Both cats became pregnant and delivered on Easter Sunday. We gave all the kittens away except one. Our family loves the story *A Christmas Carol* by Charles Dickens, so we named the baby kitten Fezziwig, after a character in the story.

When Fezzi almost died the first time, we rushed him to the hospital. The doctor thought Fezzi had cancer because his lungs were filled with fluid, but he said that he would try one more procedure. He kept him overnight. The next morning we were watching *A Christmas Carol* on television, and every time they mentioned Fezziwig, we cried. Then the phone rang, and the doctor said that the procedure had worked and that Fezzi was fine.

Some time later, Fezziwig became ill again. I was getting dressed, and I heard him coughing. I thought that he was coughing up a hairball because he had done that before. But he kept coughing, so I screamed for my daughter because I knew he was in trouble. I even tried to breathe for him, in an attempt to get the hairball out, but he was suffering from something worse than a hairball. He died in my arms on the way to the vet. The vet said that a blood clot had traveled into his lung. Fezziwig had been fine prior to his death. If he had been sick, I would have been expecting his death and would have been prepared for it, but I had no reason to expect anything. It was a painful blow. I felt like I had let him down because I couldn't save him.

I sat in a rocking chair at the veterinarian's office for about an hour holding Fezzi before I would let the staff take him away. I wanted Fezziwig to wake up and come back. I didn't know how I was going to go on because he meant so much to me.

The people in the veterinarian's office were very kind. I ran into the office wearing my nightgown and bathrobe. They called my husband, and I sat there until he arrived. My husband sat with me and cried too, although he wasn't as upset as I was. I can't remember ever being that distraught. Then we said good-bye to Fezzi. My husband helped them take him from me.

After Fezziwig died, I didn't do anything. I didn't eat. I lay on the couch and cried for three days. His death happened during our summer vacation, so I was off from work. The house was empty without Fezziwig. It was hard for me to walk down the hall where I had found him.

Fezzi helped me through some tough times. I would pet him and talk to him. I don't know if I would have made it without having him to come home to. I understand why many experts tell older people to have pets and why having pets is therapeutic. Pets help a lot.

When my husband lost his job, I had to go back to work. I cried every day on my way to work and wondered if it was worth it. Fezziwig kept me going. I felt that I had to be there for Fezziwig. I had to take care of him. I didn't feel that anybody would love him enough or be able to take care of him except me.

We had Fezziwig cremated, and I had a sarcophagus made by a lady in San Francisco. She made it to look like him. I could not put the ashes in the sarcophagus because it would have been too painful for me. My husband had to do it. Sometimes I sit and hold the sarcophagus and talk to Fezziwig. It may sound stupid, but I tell him that I think about him and miss him. I'll sit in the living room and hold the sarcophagus so I can be close to him again.

I have a little velvet box that contains all of Fezziwig's baby teeth and whiskers. For the first few months after he was gone, holding the box made me feel comfortable. Whenever I hear Elton John sing "Blue Eyes," I cry because Fezziwig had blue eyes.

Fezziwig was my baby. He was our child. He slept in our bed. Although he wasn't an extremely affectionate cat, he would lick my nose. Late at night when I was watching television by myself, Fezzi would find me, and we would have our special time together.

I had always said that if I ever lost my cats, I would want another kitten immediately. So three days after Fezziwig died, my daughter-in-law and my son showed me a picture of a Persian and said, "That's your cat, Mom. You can pick him up this afternoon at 2:30 P.M."

I went to get the cat, and at first I thought that he was ugly. I had never had a Persian before, and Persians don't have much of a nose. When the lady handed him to me, he put his paws around my neck and laid his head on my shoulders. I took him home.

When he was in our bed that night and I was petting him, he licked my nose. I cried. To me, for that one moment, it was as if Fezzi was saying, Goodbye. It's okay. You can have another cat. It was the strangest thing, because I was thinking about Fezziwig and how he used to lick my nose, then Dudley, the new Persian, was licking my nose. He has never done it since.

Even though I had a new cat, I still felt a certain amount of guilt. When Fezzi died, I wished I had spent more time with him. I wished I had brushed him more. I have tried to set aside special times together with Dudley. For example, instead of vacuuming the floor, I will sit for five minutes and brush him. He's worth it.

What saved me after my great loss was adopting Dudley right away. The first night was hard, but after he licked my nose, it was okay. I felt a calm feeling. I felt I could let go.

I think pets go to heaven like people. I believe our pets wait for us, and I think I will see Fezziwig again when I die.

There are times when I am driving home that I think of Fezziwig and cry. I still miss him. When I hear or see something that reminds me of him, I still weep. As much as I love Dudley, I will never love him the same way I loved Fezzi.

I received several sympathy cards when Fezziwig died, including cards from his regular vet and from the vet where we took him when he died. That meant a lot to me.

I have a very dear friend who sat with me for a while after Fezzi died. She also sent me a beautiful card. She didn't have pets because her husband was allergic, but we were close, and she understood what I was going through.

When my uncle put his dog down, I felt it was right to send him a card because people had sent them to me. I don't think people usually think about gestures like that, but the loss of a pet is like having a death in the family.

I've learned that no matter how much I loved Fezzi, I could never be without a pet. Having one is that important to me. I need to have something to hold onto.

I loved Fezzi so much that I never would have let him suffer. I would have put him to sleep first. I feel that way about any animal. It even bothers me to see a squirrel dead on the road.

Some people say, "Oh, I couldn't go through that again. I couldn't have another pet." But I don't know what I would have done without Dudley. I've always known that no matter how much the loss hurts, the love the pets give me is worth more than the pain.

On my piano I have a collection of cat statues that my children have bought for me. I have about twenty of them that look like Fezzi, so it's as if I'm looking at him all the time.

I think people who love cats love them despite their independent nature. Cats may seem like they are independent, but I think they need us. Dudley needs me. If I'm not in bed at night, he comes looking for me.

Dudley sleeps between our pillows, and he mashes his face against mine. If I'm turned away, he will pull my hair with his teeth until I turn around and face him. He lies with his nose against mine, purring and pushing as hard as he can. He's affectionate and I love him, but not in the same way I loved Fezzi. There will never be another Fezzi.

Ginger and Hank

AS REMEMBERED BY

Thomas R. Mowery, D.V.M.

"Pet owners who decide to put their pets to sleep should be treated with respect because it is something they have thought about at length and is difficult for them."

After graduating from college, I lived with my parents for about a year. In April 1977 my brother moved out of the house, and in May I moved out. In June my father was diagnosed with cancer, and he died in August. Everybody was gone, and my mother was alone.

Someone brought a little Labrador mix named Ginger to my office, and I decided to give her to Mom for Christmas. I felt that Mom should have a companion.

Ginger would usually stay in the house or in the garage, but she went wherever Mom went. Ginger became Mom's constant companion.

In 1991 my mother was diagnosed with terminal cancer. She worried about what would happen to Ginger. Since I couldn't see any other option, I told Mom that I would keep Ginger.

In February of 1992 my mother died, and within a week Ginger moved in with us. She walked into the house and made herself at home. Ginger was sixteen years old. We kept her for about a year and a half, and the first year we had no problems with her.

When dogs grow old, they begin to have physical problems like people. Ginger couldn't see very well because she had cataracts, so she would fall when she tried to walk upstairs. She also would urinate in the house. We couldn't get mad at her because she didn't have any control of the situation, and there was no medication that would help. We tried everything, but we couldn't be with her 100 percent of the time.

I know that if Mom had been alive, she would have wanted me to put Ginger to sleep. A person who has pets has certain responsibilities and this is one of them. I knew putting Ginger to sleep was going to be hard, but I had to do it. It was my responsibility. I felt it wasn't fair to Ginger to have her continue living in this manner. We had no choice.

As a vet, I had taken care of Ginger all her life, so I felt that I should be the one to put her to sleep. I had always said that I would let someone else do it, but when it came down to it, I had to do it myself.

While the decision was very hard for me, I knew that it was the right decision. The only thing that I did wrong was that I did not make the decision soon enough. When I told the kids that we needed to put Ginger down, they were very upset and cried. I cried too, but I held firm.

I buried Ginger by the strawberry patch at my mother's place where Ginger liked to sleep while my mom picked strawberries. The children went with me that day. After the burial, we had no special ceremony; the kids and I just talked about Ginger being with Grandma.

When my dad died, I still had Mom. When my mom died, I had Ginger. When I put Ginger down, it brought back memories of Mom and Dad, so Ginger's death was very hard for me. I wanted to keep Ginger's collar, but I didn't. I believe life must go on. I am not saying that we should never look back, but we must look forward.

We had another Labrador named Hank that we had to put to sleep after Ginger. When we moved to the country, my wife, Deb, wanted a dog for protection, so we got Hank. We adopted him when he was eight months old. He was given to us by friends because he had grown too big for their house.

Hank was good with the kids, especially with our little girl, Casey. Hank would tolerate anything and everything from the children. They were very close to him. Deb and I both worked, but the children had Hank to play with.

As Hank grew older, he had trouble getting up and down by himself. He would lie down in the yard and then couldn't get up. Although he had a few good days, he had several physical problems because of his age.

We told the kids that we would not make the decision of putting Hank to sleep unless all four of us agreed to it. It was a family decision.

The children had a more difficult time giving up Hank than Ginger because we had Ginger for only a year and a half, and we had Hank for thirteen years. The main reason the children felt bad about losing Ginger was because they knew she was Grandma's dog.

Casey was closer to Hank than anybody. She was only eight years old when we had to make the decision, and she said that we should do it. She understood why we had to put him to sleep.

Casey wanted to hold Hank before he was put to sleep. We had Hank cremated, and Casey wanted to keep his ashes, which we have in the pantry. We plan to sprinkle his ashes on his favorite paths that he took everyday to the neighbors' houses to get snacks.

Professionally, I feel that euthanasia is necessary. Some people think that euthanasia is evil, but there is nothing wrong with death, even though people in our society see it as a taboo. I look at it in two ways. Some animals are not adoptable, and they should be euthanized. For other animals, we are putting them out of their pain or prolonged suffering.

When it comes to sick animals and old animals, I believe that part of my oath as a veterinarian is to provide them relief from their pain. We can't heal old age or terminal illnesses. In some ways, we are kinder to animals than we are to our fellow human beings.

Some people come into my office and act as if they don't care. They will say that it is just a dog. They want us to take care of it and send them the bill. They don't even stay until it's over.

Most people, though, who come into our hospital want what is best for their animals. Sometimes people bring in pets that are severely arthritic and are having trouble getting up and down, but they don't know if it is time to put their animals to sleep. I tell them that when the time comes, they will know. I tell people that euthanasia is a decision that they have to make, and once they make it, the decision cannot be reversed. I never tell them when to put a pet to sleep. Many times they will say, "You know, Doc, you were right. It became too painful. We did not have a choice." At this stage, I feel the clients have accepted their decision.

I offer the pet owners the choice of whether to stay in the room during the euthanasia or not. I explain the procedure to them so it won't be a shock. I also present options of what we can do with their pets after the euthanasia.

When children come into the clinic, I tell them that they are welcome to be present, but if they choose not to, it is okay. Some want to stay and others don't. I don't push the issue either way because I don't know if there is a right or wrong answer.

After the euthanasia, many clients cry and say that it was the hardest decision they ever had to make. Some pet owners say, "It would have been so nice to have come downstairs and found her dead. We could have buried her and that would have been great, but when we had to make the decision, we felt so guilty."

I am very emotional, and I will get tears in my eyes after an animal has been put to sleep. There is nothing wrong with crying. I try to do it in a dignified, professional manner.

Pet owners who decide to put their pets to sleep should be treated with respect because it is something they have thought about at length and is difficult for them.

I feel sad for the animals, but I also feel sad for the people because I know how they feel. Sometimes I'll see someone who has lost a spouse, and now he or she is losing the pet they shared together. I had a client whose husband was diagnosed with terminal cancer and had six months to live. A week later, her dog was diagnosed with cancer. She experienced a tremendous amount of grief with the loss of her husband and her dog.

We don't offer counseling, but I try to support my clients. I answer their questions if they have any. We sometimes send a bouquet of flowers to say that we are thinking of them. I treat people how I would want to be treated. I think most people go through all the stages of grieving, but some people never show it.

I tell my clients that there is nothing wrong with talking to children about death. Children accept death better than we think. I don't think they understand about life and death, but they are willing to accept death.

For example, when my daughter, Casey, was three years old, our cat, Snickers, died. Since he died in January, we could not bury him because it was too cold. We wrapped Snickers in a blanket and put him in the playhouse. In March, when it was warmer, we buried him under a tree near the barn. Later Casey asked if we could dig up Snickers. She had no concept of what death really was because she was very young.

On the other hand, my parents never talked to me about death. I was ten when my fourteen-year-old sister died, and my parents never talked about her death. One summer my sister was diagnosed with leukemia, and the following summer she died. My parents never told me that she was sick. I only knew that she was in the hospital.

At times I look back and wonder how I could not have realized what was happening. As a ten-year-old kid, I didn't know fear. I felt that life went on, and nothing was going to happen to me.

I grew up on a farm, so when our animals died, it was considered part of life. I can remember burying our cats when I was a kid. We had lambs, cows, and cats that died, and I don't remember seeing death as being bad.

The first time I talked about death was with my grandmother when I was eighteen. Now I can talk about death in general and can even talk about the death of our pets, but if I had to talk about the death of one of my children with the other child, I couldn't do that. I don't think anybody could. I don't know if I would do anything different than my parents did.

I am fortunate to be in this profession. I like to help animals and their owners. One of the good aspects about being a veterinarian is that I have made many friends among my clients. I receive a lot of thank-you cards from my clients.

Once I received a call from some people who lived north of my home. They wanted their seventeen-year-old German shepherd put to sleep, but nobody from their clinic would come to their house to do it. I drove a mile and a half and put their pet to sleep. The people kept thanking me and even sent me a thank-you note. About two weeks later, they transferred the care of all their animals over to our office. They said that they had spent a lot of money over the years, but when they needed the clinic, the people there wouldn't come.

What it comes down to for me is that life is a gift. What we do with that gift is our choice, and we only have one chance. I enjoy each day and I do my best at work and at home. My family is my first priority, but my job as a veterinarian is important too.

Rebel

AS REMEMBERED BY

Jeffrey Frischkorn

"The ceremony was my final tribute to Rebel. . . . The importance of the ceremony was that it was the final act of honoring a friend."

Rebel was six months old when I bought him at a Ducks Unlimited auction. Some party revelers at the event fed Rebel some alcohol, and he lapped it up. Throughout his life, Rebel was willing to eat anything, but the alcohol made him very ill. He proceeded to throw up.

I saw a lot of redeeming qualities in that pup. We hit it off right away and became very good friends—as much as a dog and a human can be.

Rebel was a rambunctious puppy. During the first few months when my family and I weren't at home, we kept him in a dog crate. The idea that dogs don't make messes in their own bedding was a joke with him because he had no problem doing that. He often created work for our daughter and us.

Rebel was a dog whom almost everybody in the neighborhood enjoyed. He would bark at people who came to the door, but if he was in the yard, people could go up to him and pet him. A couple of times he escaped into the community, and we would have to go down the street and hunt for him. One time we found him with some young kids who had him all dressed up in doll clothes. He sat there as happy as a lark.

While Rebel wasn't vicious or mean by any stretch of the imagination, he went to his grave hating skunks with a passion. He would get into a fight at least once a year with a skunk and always lost, but he never learned his lesson. We had to keep antiskunk chemicals that we called "skunk juice."

He was a friend and a member of the family. We would take him to picnics, on camping trips, for swims, and for walks.

When I had pneumonia in one lung and was hacking away, Rebel came running into the room and put his chin on the bed. As much as one can think of a dog having a concerned and sympathetic look, he did. He lay there until I went to sleep.

As the outdoors writer for the paper, I had a chance to do a lot of hunting with Rebel. I spent more time with my dog than most people do with their pets. He was a one-man dog. When he was around a group of people and I was there, he would stay with me rather than float from one person to the next. I have another Lab named Daisy and she's a sweetheart, but she could be anybody's dog. If a person petted her, she would go sit next to him as if he owned her. But Rebel was a territorial male, and he had a strong desire to spend his time with me. He would hunt with me only. Nobody else could take him out in the field if I wasn't along.

Rebel suffered severely from hip dysphasia and arthritis, which ravaged his body. For about two years he received cortisone shots every four to six weeks. The shots kept him going until the last couple months, when the frequency of treatments increased and the duration of his ability to withstand pain began to decrease.

Before the holidays a couple of family members suggested I put him down, but I said that there was no way I could do that at holiday time. I had hoped that he might make it until March, but it became very apparent in January that he only had a few weeks to live.

I knew that the decision to have Rebel put to sleep was coming. I had talked with the vet about it almost every time Rebel needed an injection. We would estimate how much longer he had to live. I could see that he was progressively becoming worse. Rebel had less and less ability to control his bodily functions. He would slip and slide. He'd be in pain. I used a heating pad for him to lay his hips on, and he appreciated it. I did everything I could to make him as comfortable as possible.

Rebel was a fighter and a trooper to the end. The vet didn't want me to take him out hunting or running, but I tried to make sure that he got out for an hour or two every couple of weeks simply because he enjoyed the thrill.

The hunting dog—master relationship is a unique and close bond. The dog doesn't just sit beside the master during an evening while the master scratches his ears. The master is outdoors in a natural environment with the dog for a long time. I strongly believe that hunting dogs should be house dogs. The best way for an animal to bond with a master is to spend as much time as possible together. I think that's vital for a working dog or a hunting dog. I would take trips with Rebel, and we would be gone for a couple of days. He'd be there in the motel room or at the campsite. He was a constant companion.

I chose cremation for Rebel partly because of the time of the year. In February I would have had difficulty digging a hole. The other reason was location. I lived in a suburb, and I simply couldn't go out in my backyard and bury my dog. I'm not sure about pet cemeteries. I'm not going to say they're wrong for some people, but I don't feel comfortable with the idea. I felt cremation with a ceremony would be the most appropriate manner in which to honor Rebel.

The crematorium that I chose in downtown Cleveland is a human crematorium, but it has a separate facility for pets. I took Rebel there very late on a Sunday and was astounded by the courtesy I received. The people were every bit as sympathetic as a funeral director. By coincidence, a person who works at the crematorium lives near my home, so that person was kind enough to bring the cremains in a box to my home.

The people went out of their way to be accommodating, and they did it in very quick order.

My wife, who is very handy with woodworking, said that she would create a wooden urn in which I could store Rebel's ashes. I made a brass plaque for it. I had a photo of Rebel enlarged, framed, and matted. I took two locks of his hair and had the framer put one of the locks of hair between the glass and the matting. The photo hangs over my gun cabinet. Whenever I pass by, I see a lovely gold frame and tan matting with Rebel's mustard-colored fur. I have a friend who ties flies, so I'm going to have him tie a couple of special flies made from Rebel's hair that I will not use.

I was emotionally devastated by the loss of my dog. I took the entire day to rough out a column about Rebel on a Monday, and I am known at the paper as an extremely fast writer. I have never taken an entire day to write before. I reread the column every day to make some changes and corrections. It wasn't until Friday that I could reread the column without choking up. I shed a considerable amount of tears during that time. Writing the story was excellent spontaneous therapy for me.

The people at work knew what I had gone through, and they were very supportive and sympathetic. Rebel's death had not been a sudden surprise to either the readers or my coworkers at the paper. I had talked about my activities with Rebel and how his health had deteriorated. My readers knew for many years the condition that Rebel was in, and they had followed the story. In fact, a number of readers commented that when they read my column, they always looked for word on how Rebel and I were doing.

I've saved all the cards and letters of sympathy that I received from my readers after the article about his death was published. In seventeen years of outdoor writing and with a few hundred stories per year that I write, I have never received a greater outpouring or response. I received at least twenty-six letters and cards.

The letters meant a lot to me—probably more than a lot of people knew. I felt good knowing somebody who was willing to give emotional support. I was glad to know that people read my column and that they sympathized with what I had gone through, even if they were not dog owners. The words of sympathy helped keep me from becoming remote and distant from others.

My wife has been a strong support to me. She was Rebel's good buddy too. We've been married almost twenty-four years, so she was there with Rebel from day one. His death hit her very hard. She hasn't objected to anything that I have done— neither the expense of cremation nor the rituals that I determined I wanted to use to honor the dog. She thought that the photograph I have with the lock of hair was very good.

For about a week after Rebel's death, Daisy appeared to be disoriented. She would wander about the house and sit down where Rebel normally would, then she would get up and move off. We have a cat named Inky who was good friends with Rebel. The two were about the same age and had grown up together. Inky appeared to wonder where her friend was.

I have Rebel's collar hanging up, and it will never go on another dog. On the night he passed away, I took his stainless steel food dish and turned it upside down. It has stayed that way to this day. It will not be used again until I get another dog. My wife has not moved that dish or slid it out of the way.

Bereavement is vital. Some people become too maudlin and cannot go on. They may even say that they don't want to go through that experience again so they are not going to have another dog. I think they deprive themselves of the joy of owning a pet.

I focused on the good times. Rebel and I had good times up to the end. The picture of Rebel with the lock of hair is a reminder of the good times we had and a reminder of the challenge of training the dog.

On the day that I decided to conduct my memorial for Rebel at the club where we hunted, I had some errands to do, so I combined the two trips. I did not take Daisy, my other dog. I went alone. I don't think I would have done the ceremony had anybody else been present at the club. I would have gone back another day.

I had hoped to complete the ceremony earlier, but the weather didn't cooperate. I finally saw a window of opportunity between rain showers, so I went ahead and did it. I had loaded two shotgun shells with Rebel's ashes at home. That was more emotional than anything else—putting some of Rebel's ashes into the shotgun shells.

I sat on the only rock in the area and read Cory Ford's "The Road to Tinkhamtown," which many believe is the definitive piece of outdoor writing. It is a very moving story about the passing of an old man and his dog. The story is about the merging of the two and their reacquaintance after death. The reading got me misty eyed. I proceeded to blow a dog whistle. That was probably the emotional high point.

Following the reading and the blowing of the whistle, I fired two rounds out of the shotgun, which spread Rebel's ashes across the grounds at the club where he and I did a lot of our walking and hunts together. I have the two empty shells, and I will never reuse them for any kind of shooting. The whole ceremony took less than thirty minutes.

The ceremony was my final tribute to Rebel. The majority of tears and emotions were expended when he died. As I sat on the rock, I thought about the good times I shared with Rebel. The importance of the ceremony was that it was the final act of honoring a friend. It was something that I promised to do. I vowed that I was going to do it for myself, and I did. I felt better that I had kept my word.

I also planted a flowering dogwood tree in my backyard, and I poured some of Rebel's ashes into the hole. Whenever I see it, I remember Rebel. In fact, my wife and I refer to it as "Rebel's Tree."

I view the death of a human to be more of a religious experience. My fundamental Christian belief is that human beings have souls and an afterlife, but animals do not. I accept that without question, but it does not diminish the loss that I feel for the dog. The death of an animal does not have the religious connotation that the loss of my father or the loss of a close relative does. Even though my relationship with Rebel was substantial, the loss is a replaceable one. I can get another dog, but I cannot get another father, nor would I want to.

I have no qualms about buying another dog, and I know I'm going to have to go through the routine of training a dog again. Rebel serves as a reminder of the good times and the difficult work of training another dog. I realize I'll have to go through the loss again—I'll have to go through it with Daisy. But the pain is more than compensated for by the companionship that the dog provides.

I would tell other pet owners to prepare themselves and not to think that the loss won't happen. They should accept the inevitable. They should talk frequently with a veterinarian and find out as much as they can about their dogs' particular ailments and what their options are. Death is going to hit a person harder whose animal passes away suddenly and unexpectedly.

I had two years to prepare for Rebel's death, and that probably helped me get through it the best. I didn't delay his death longer than I should have. I knew it was going to happen.

Wizard

AS REMEMBERED BY

Tara Cohen

*"Don't let anybody tell you how to grieve because you'll
have your own process of grieving. If you need help, ask for it."*

My grieving began about a month and a half before
Wizard died when cancer reared its ugly head in the
form of a grossly distended liver. The following weeks
of tests, diets, pills, prayers, and tears were an unbefitting end for
her. Even as Wizard grew weak from liver cancer and couldn't
eat, her sweet disposition never left her.

When she couldn't fight it anymore, I cradled her in my arms
all the way to the emergency vet. She was barely able to move.
She pulled through the night, while I cried, prayed, and hoped
that a phone call wouldn't come to say that she was gone.

The next day my husband and I spent over an hour with her,
saying goodbye. To give her some dignity, I had the vet remove
her IV and make her as comfortable as possible. She seemed
ready to go, and I didn't want to make her suffer anymore. No
matter what we did, the cancer would win.

As the vet gave her the deadly medicine, I held her in my
arms and stroked her lovingly and whispered, "I love you,"
over and over. She closed her eyes, and her head fell. I was
alone with her for quite a while after she was gone. I arranged
her body on a pillow, brushed her, and covered her so she

looked as though she were taking a nap. Her fur and towels were wet with my tears, but they seemed to add a brightness to her coat.

This was the first time I had handled the dead body of a loved one. I had refused to do it in the past. It was extremely painful, but it helped me to touch that once-warm, loving body because it made me realize that she was gone.

I had Wizard cremated because that is what I want for myself. I see no use in keeping the body because the body is useless when the soul is gone. A few weeks later I picked up her ashes at the vet's, and I sat in the car, grieving and holding the ashes.

A few days later I went out in the bitter cold and spread her ashes over a field of pussy willows near our home where I had put Merlyn, my other cat. While tears poured down my face, I prayed and sang a song for Wizard. I don't know if the ceremony was more for my own comfort or hers. I don't remember the words.

I wanted to let her go because I do believe that animals have souls, and that keeps me going. I also believe that someday I will meet her and the others again. I believe she is in heaven. We had three other cats at the time. Tasha had been with Wizard for thirteen years and kept looking for her. The other cats also missed her. They would go to her favorite spots and look for her, but she wasn't there.

After my mom died, I went through several years of emotional upheaval. Wizard was there for me whenever I needed her. She would be at my side and would give me a kiss or do something silly to make me laugh.

Wizard was my kid. I had 3-D photos taken of her. I have one hanging downstairs. It's mostly of her head and her torso, so it is close to life size. Whenever one of the cats sees it, he's startled. He won't even get close enough to smell it.

I had the vet clip a little bit of her fur. I also have the cards that people sent us. The cards acknowledged that the senders understood my loss.

When Wizard died, I was overwhelmed with grief. I knew the end was coming, otherwise I would have lost control. Wizard was such an intricate part of my life. She was the only connection I had to my past, to where I was born. When she died, it was like a piece of me was missing—another piece that goes along with my mom.

Although I knew that Wizard was gone, I would still look for her. She used to sleep next to me in bed, so for a while I thought she was still there.

When Wizard died, I didn't go to work for two days. My coworkers knew what was going on, and if they didn't understand, that was their problem. Previously, I had gone to work after a loss, but I decided I wasn't going to do that again.

I had the usual anger because Wizard was gone, but I wasn't mad at Wizard. After my mom passed away, I had done some reading about grief. I knew the phases. As far as I was concerned, Wizard didn't deserve to suffer. I don't think any animal deserves that.

During the year after Wizard died, I would remember her and start to cry. I'd go in the family room and shut the door to be by myself. I will always cry. I know that I can't change the situation, and I can't bring her back. Part of acceptance is that you have to live and continue on. You can't curl up and die. To live and be happy, you have to accept death. You have to work through the grief.

After Wizard died, I made sure another animal was with me. It is important to me that I have animals around. I've had times in my life, such as when I was in school, when I couldn't have animals. So I would go to the houses of other people and pet their animals. Animals are a passion in my life.

My husband was my support during my loss of Wizard. He had a hard time too. It was the first time he had experienced a loss of any animal. I also had a couple of friends with whom I would talk about my loss.

I called a grief counselor who lived quite a distance away and talked to her for a few minutes. The counselor listened to me. I think that's what I needed—somebody to listen. She wasn't able to suggest a counselor who lived closer. I make sure to tell people that when they lose somebody, they can call on me. I'll listen because I know how important it is.

The one dream that I remember the most was the one that started in an apartment where we once lived. I was sitting on the couch, and I saw Wizard outside the window. I opened the window and she came in, but she didn't have any eyes. She sat by me. In front of me, there was a very tall, good-looking man in a white coat. I had no idea who he was.

He asked me about Wizard. He said things like "Oh, that's a nice cat." I said that he didn't understand. I told him that Wizard was dead and was not supposed to be here. He carried on as if there was nothing wrong with that. Wizard was sitting on my left side where she always sat. I had my arm around her, and I was petting her.

I remember the man in the dream saying, "You did all you could." Wizard also spoke in the dream. She said, "Everything's fine."

I thought if I kept my eyes closed, the dream would continue. There was a pause, and the dream stopped. I was petting somebody next to me. When I looked down, it was my Bengal who sleeps in the same position that Wizard did and is as sweet as her. She has the same black, brown, and gold colorings.

The dream upset me because it seemed so real. I tried to analyze why Wizard didn't have any eyes. The only reason I could figure out is that it wasn't her because her soul wasn't there. I had always looked into Wizard's eyes the way I look into people's eyes. I can tell a lot about individuals that way.

From the loss of Wizard, I've learned that I am stronger than I thought. I can handle loss. When my mother died, I tried to commit suicide. But that's something I wouldn't even think about now. Not that I wouldn't do it for my cat, but I understand that it is just desperation. And I won't let myself reach that point anymore because I've grown.

I would tell others to enjoy the time they have with their animals and to do the best that they can for their health. When the time comes, grieve. Don't let anybody tell you how to grieve because you'll have your own process of grieving. If you need help, ask for it.

What helped me was talking, sharing, writing, having the other animals around, having the dream, and reading about loss. I wrote something to Wizard, but I didn't keep it. I used to keep my writings, but they were too painful to read, so I would write to get the feelings out of my system and then throw the paper away. I wrote things like "I miss you. I wish you were here."

Wizard is up with my mom, and she is better off. I know that one day I'm going to see her again. I want her to have fun while she is there. I am glad she is out of pain.

My husband found some phone numbers of pet loss support lines on the Internet as well as poems that people have left. We copied some of the poems. We talked to people on the computer who shared their stories.

I think grief is grief. If the animal or person that passed away was close to you and meant a lot to you, then you need to grieve. You are going to grieve whether someone else validates your feelings or not.

My grief has gone through all the stages. Sometimes I think acceptance is the hardest part because I have to continue to do my best to live this life even though a piece of my heart is missing.

Schnooky

AS REMEMBERED BY

Deborah J. Prisco

"If you suppress your grief and don't let it out, then the unfinished work will come back and haunt you."

Schnooky was the light of my life from the time I found her on June 21, 1977, until October 11, 1994, when she died. She was the only source of unconditional love that I have ever experienced. When Schnooky came into my life, I decided to give life a chance.

My childhood, adolescence, and adulthood were devoid of nurturing relationships until the tiny four-week-old mixed-breed puppy and I found each other. She had been abandoned on a road near an auto repair shop where my car had been towed. Schnooky limped into the service station, scared, malnourished, and trembling. It was love at first sight for me. Having her nuzzle in my arms made my wrecked car seem less important. Giving Schnooky a home was my first unselfish act in a long time.

Schnooky and I shared a lot of special times together. On Sundays when she was little, I would take her to Dairy Queen because she loved soft vanilla ice cream in a regular cone. She didn't like the sugar cones. Schnooky would get her own ice-cream cone, and I would get mine.

We would go for walks. My husband and I also would take Schnooky in our boat out to a sand bar in the Gulf that is about two miles long, and Schnooky would run and chase the sea gulls.

We took Schnooky on every trip we ever went on. One of our favorite trips was visiting my mother-in-law in Bricktown, New Jersey. She was eighty-three years old and was not a dog person, but when she and Schnooky met, they fell in love with one another.

The first time Schnooky received a professional haircut, I cried. It was like taking my kid to the barber for the first time. Schnooky and I would watch Oprah's talk show. One day we were watching Oprah and she told a poignant story about people like my family, and I started to cry. Schnooky crawled up onto my lap to comfort me. I grew up in a dysfunctional family. I am one of those characters who never knew what parental love was suppose to be because the children in our family were an afterthought.

Since my mother married several times, we moved around a lot when I was a child. She was fond of cats, but whenever we would move, the cats were abandoned. Many of the cats she had were sick because they never received the proper care. To my mother, the cats had no value, so I grew up being devastated and crying for days whenever we had to leave one.

I never had anyone who loved just me. Schnooky loved only me, and it was the greatest gift. She would love me even when I was in a bad mood. If I forgot to feed her, she would still love me. We were best friends.

We were like mother and daughter. Schnooky was the mother and I was the daughter. Schnooky was a patient teacher and a friend. She taught me how to love and how to live. She taught me responsibility. She taught me that animals, children, and even I have value. She was the best friend I ever had. Schnooky gave me unconditional love.

My devoted friend touched many lives. Quite by accident, she became a therapy dog. I frequently brought her to the office because of my work schedule. Once she assisted my business partner, Greg, in his psychotherapy practice by greeting a client who had arrived for counseling. The pooch made herself at home on the couch next to the woman. Schnooky was so well received by the patient that we allowed her to remain in our office. People began to request her presence during their sessions, and we complied.

Schnooky became the official volunteer pet for the local hospice house. The patients in the hospice house are terminal with a prognosis of thirty days or less. When patients come to the hospice house to spend their last days, they sometimes have had to leave family pets with loved ones or in a local animal shelter.

Petting and loving Schnooky soothed the patients. By lessening their anxiety over the separation from their familiar surroundings, they were able to make their transition out of this life and into the next with less worry. The hospice employees also benefited by having Schnooky around. They experienced less tension on the job after a few minutes of nuzzling and scuffing with the fur ball.

Schnooky was my best friend. I never thought about her being mortal until her stroke in September of 1993. I was devastated.

The vet said that Schnooky was the most amazing and courageous little dog that he had ever treated. Her will to live was evidenced by her quick recovery. For the next few months she thrived, but eventually old age took its toll.

I denied she was failing for months. She couldn't jump on the bed or on the futon that was on the patio. Schnooky was miserable. When she wasn't sleeping in a nearly comatose state, she would walk about the house in so much pain.

I took Schnooky on one last ride to the vet's office and had her euthanized on October 11, 1994. She was eighteen years old and had renal failure. My grief was overwhelming. My body was numb while I held her and they gave her the lethal injection. Then in one instant she was gone. Through my tears,

I asked her to forgive me if taking her life at that moment was the wrong thing to do.

I pleaded for her spirit to go toward the loving light into her next spiritual life. I sang our favorite song, "You Are My Sunshine." I kissed all four of her paws. I held her until she was cold and motionless, then I said goodbye. It never occurred to me how final her death would be. One moment she was warm and fuzzy, and then within seconds she was gone—she was absolutely gone.

The thought of losing her forever was almost unbearable. I thought about suicide at that moment so I could join her because I felt so horrible. I felt abandonment, guilt, and punishment for something that I had done or not done. I stayed in my bed for three days. The only reason that I got up for was to use the toilet and feed my cats, then I would go back to bed. I wouldn't eat because I had no appetite. It was almost as if I had died.

I had a lot of anger, and I took it out on everybody around me. I was very irritable. I didn't want to be bothered. I didn't want anybody around me. I wanted everyone to disappear so I could have my dog back.

I bargained with God when Schnooky was very sick. I prayed that if he would make her better, I would try to be the best person in the world. I wouldn't drink Pepsi anymore. I vowed that I would watch my health better because I am a cancer patient. I promised all those things if he would let her be okay.

When I was thirty-six years old, I was diagnosed with cancer. I felt more pain when Schnooky died than I did when I was diagnosed. The chemotherapy was a mere inconvenience compared to the pain I felt when she died.

I realized that it was best to let her go so she wouldn't be in any pain, but I missed her so much. I felt like I had betrayed her. After she died, there was a tremendous void in my heart.

I wanted her death to be special and loving because I believe in an afterlife. Schnooky has gone on, and she is doing someone else a wonderful favor by being their pet. I wasn't afraid of losing Schnooky because I know that we will be together again.

When Schnooky didn't come home, one of my cats, Phoebe, developed quite an aversion to me and the other cats in the house. Schnooky and Phoebe had been inseparable. Phoebe would snuggle with Schnooky all the time, and they slept in a pile together. Schnooky would climb up in bed with me, and Phoebe would lie on Schnooky and lick her face.

After Schnooky passed away, Phoebe would look for her and cry. She would sniff Schnooky's blanket and her bedding. I tried to get rid of most of the stuff that had Schnooky's scent. Phoebe would sit at the door and cry. She was definitely depressed after Schnooky died.

I feel that I have accepted Schnooky's death because death is as much a part of living as birth is. I have moments when I hear her bark, but it's another dog across the way. There are moments when I feel her presence or smell her fur. She had a wonderful natural scent.

This was not the first time that I had experienced death. In the past three years, I have lost two good friends to AIDS, but their deaths occurred in progressive stages. I knew what was happening, and I prepared. There have been a couple of shocking deaths in my family. One of my brothers committed suicide.

The difference between grieving for a pet and grieving for a human being is that grieving for a pet is more intimate. It's much more painful. Humans have control over most aspects of their lives, and they have responsibility for what happens. Pets neither think about yesterday nor do they project into the future—so they live in the here and now. They have no thoughts about death.

It's acceptable to be angry and to go through the stages of grief for the loss of a pet, but our society does not accept pet death as it accepts human death. I think most people don't give enough importance to pet death. They say, "Oh, get another cat or another dog." Some people feel that animals don't have the same value that human life has. I feel that pets are more valuable than humans because they give us much more.

I did not expect the outpouring of condolences my family received. Sympathy cards and letters from friends and clients poured in. Strangers who saw Schnooky during her daily walks around the neighborhood sent cards. At the office, people fought back their tears when they heard of Schnooky's passing.

Everyone at the veterinarian's office were caring and understanding. The veterinarians and the assistants loved animals, and they had taken care of Schnooky for thirteen years, so she was part of the family at the vet's office.

My husband, Art, was devastated by Schnooky's death. He interrupted an important business meeting to come home and be with me when I told him that Schnooky was gone. He is still grieving.

My former husband, Rick, who is a good friend of the family, cried for two weeks. He sent encouraging messages and wanted to be present when we dispersed her ashes on her favorite beach.

The veterinarians, James Powell and Jerry Reed, of All Pets Hospital arranged for her cremation and sent flowers with a warm message from all the staff. Their office manager, Patty, called Schnooky's former vet nurse in Mississippi. Connie was Schnooky's primary vet nurse during her illnesses and had grown fond of the pup. She phoned me and soothed my emotional wounds. My guilt subsided because all these wonderful people cared enough to help.

The first therapy that I had was one-on-one individual grief therapy, and it was healing. I usually suppressed a lot of emotions, but I finally let out my tears.

We do grief therapy every day at the hospice, and that helped me. I met with four of my friends, and we formed our own support group, which continues to meet. I would have survived without the support, but it wouldn't have been easy because a lot of these people are a big part of my life.

My personal advice to pet owners who are grieving for a beloved pet is to consult with their veterinarian. If your veterinarian is not sympathetic to your emotional needs, then find one who is. There are also a lot of good books on human grief. I believe that the grief is exactly the same when you lose your pet.

Pet owners should also seek counseling. If you can't cry, then get some counseling until you can cry. If you suppress your grief and don't let it out, then the unfinished work will come back and haunt you. I have a neighbor whose dog died in her husband's arms, and after many years he is still torn up with pain. He refuses to pet another animal and won't even talk about it. It is such a waste of love.

I have Schnooky's ashes, and I'm going to wait until the summer when my former husband can come from Dallas to have a ceremony. He used to come and see Schnooky every year. They had a great relationship. He loved the dog. In fact, our divorce decree allowed him visitations.

We are planning to have a Native American ceremonial purification. My partner, Greg, has Native American in his heritage, and he knows a lot about smudging and sacred smoke and spirit animals. We will sprinkle some tobacco and corn meal to honor Schnooky's spirit.

I kept Schnooky's collar and a chewed ball that she had for thirteen years. I have her blanket that she loved to sleep on. I saved her tennis bracelet with rhinestones that I bought for her sixteenth birthday. She looked pretty when she wore her jewelry.

I treated Schnooky the way that I wish I had been treated when I was growing up. I gave her all the love that I didn't get. I gave her all the special treats that I never got. She was the baby that I never had. I was nurturing my own soul by nurturing her. Schnooky helped me appreciate my own life.

The greatest joy and the most important lessons I've learned in this lifetime came from Schnooky. She was the truest source of unconditional love. My grief will run its natural course. The pain is eased when I remember what a great life Schnooky and I had together. She was my soul mate, so I know she will be waiting for me when it is my time to go toward the light.

Cookie Marie

AS REMEMBERED BY

Linda Carroll

*"While you can't replace the pet that you lost,
you can learn to love the new one."*

I was a volunteer for the humane society for about seven years. Sometimes I would take in strays and try to find homes for them. Since we didn't have a shelter, the volunteers would offer foster care for the homeless animals in their own homes.

One day I volunteered to handle the hot line for the humane society, and I received a call from a lady who said that she needed to find a home for a toy Chihuahua. The lady didn't want the dog because she would mess up the floor whenever the woman left her in the house alone all day. I decided to find the dog a new home, so I had my daughter drive over and pick her up.

The dog was not much bigger than a rat and weighed about three pounds. There are some larger breeds of Chihuahuas, but she was tiny. She ran around our house and jumped over the furniture. She looked like she was right at home. At that moment I knew I would be keeping her forever. Since my daughter's middle name is Marie, my husband called this little tiny dog "Cookie Marie." She stole our hearts.

She was about twenty-two months old when she came into our home. We had five larger dogs at the time, but Cookie Marie was special. She was my baby and she was my first Chihuahua. Cookie Marie was the queen of the house. She did what she wanted. She was the boss. We waited on her hand and foot.

We played together with her toys every night. Sometimes she would wake my husband at three o'clock in the morning, and he would play with her. Sometimes I would ignore her on purpose to see what she would do. She would pick up a toy, bring it over, and press it against my hand until I played with her. After we were through playing, I would bring her a cup of water and set it on the nightstand. She would take her vitamin with her water. She was very smart. She would look over at her cup on the nightstand and start barking to remind me to get her some water. It was a ritual: she would play with her toys, take her vitamin, and then have a drink of water.

Cookie and I went everywhere together. She would sit on my shoulder and wag her tail. If we were beside another car at a red light, she would flirt with the people in the other car. Her tail would never quit wagging. She enjoyed traveling with me. Cookie even went to the bank with me once a week. She was the perfect pet.

We took walks every day around noon. I would take her out in the summer because she loved to sunbathe. She had a special little blanket that I would lay on the grass for her, and she would sunbathe for twenty minutes. If there was a stream of sunshine coming through the window, she would lie there. She loved the sunshine.

My husband and Cookie Marie were very close. If he had to go somewhere besides work, she wanted to go with him. Even when he would tell her no, she still would go out through the door and up to the truck. She would demand that he put her in the truck, and he always did. Cookie Marie loved him as much as she loved me, and my husband loved her too. She was our baby.

Cookie Marie had special meals and snacks that she loved to eat. My husband would wake up before I did, and he would heat a little snack in the microwave for her. We never gave it to her cold, and we would cut it into small pieces. As soon as the microwave bell would go off, she would start barking because she couldn't wait.

The veterinarian said that chicken and rice would be a good diet for her to gain weight. I boiled the chicken for her, which she loved to eat. Usually I had to stop fixing dinner for us to feed her because she couldn't wait. She was spoiled rotten. She would not eat dog food because she loved her chicken.

On Fridays when my husband was paying the bills, Cookie knew that we were going to the bank and to Sonic, a fast-food restaurant, and I would buy her a cheeseburger. That was a special day for her.

We loved her so much. I was her mommy, and my husband was her daddy. Every day when my husband drove up, I would say, "There's Daddy," and she would become excited. Sometimes she would hear him first, and she would look at me and wag her tail. I would look at Cookie and she would look at me and it was as if we knew what each other was thinking. She was like a human in an animal's body.

Cookie Marie loved to take baths. She was so tiny that I would bathe her in the kitchen sink, and she would sit underneath the faucet. I would use warm water and have the towel in the dryer so it would be warm. She loved to be wrapped in the warm towel. In cold weather, I would dry her with a hair dryer. She enjoyed being brushed afterward. She was bathed every two weeks and loved it. When the weather was cold, she would wear her little pink sweater.

One night when I was taking a Tums tablet for my indigestion, Cookie looked at me and I knew that she wanted a bite. She wanted to sample everything I ate. I gave her a tiny bit of it, and she loved it. So every day she would go into the kitchen and would look up at the refrigerator where I kept the Tums. I would say, "Okay, Cookie has heartburn. I have to give her a piece of Tums."

Cookie Marie was sociable. She would escort anyone who came to the door into the house. Everyone loved her company because she was so friendly. Cookie would win them over with her flirtation. She flirted with men unmercifully.

My mother said that I spoiled Cookie Marie too much. She described Cookie as having frog eyes, a button nose, and legs that were about as long as a cigarette.

I called her "Cookie the Lionhearted" because she wasn't afraid of anything. Our other pets were afraid of Cookie Marie. She was their boss. I have a female German shepherd, Babsy, who was afraid of Cookie because Cookie would bite her on the chin. Cookie meant business.

At feeding time the other animals would step aside and let Cookie Marie eat her dinner first. She would eat what she wanted, then the other animals would eat. We shouldn't have let her do that, but she was the boss.

Cookie didn't care for other animals, but she was very friendly with people. Cookie enjoyed being around children. She would lick them and play with them.

When Cookie became sick and died unexpectedly from complications of bladder stones, I was shocked and devastated. Since she was still young, I thought that she had a long life ahead of her.

One Monday morning Cookie was acting funny, so I took her to the vet. He wasn't my regular vet because I was living in Florida temporarily. Cookie Marie couldn't urinate, and the vet didn't know what was wrong with her. He sent her home after keeping her for a few hours and giving her medication.

I kept her home for another twenty-four hours, but she was only lying there. I called the vet and told him that he had to do something—Cookie was not getting better. I took her back to him.

On Wednesday afternoon, the vet took x-rays and found the problem. I was thankful that he was going to do something for her. Around five o'clock in the afternoon he said that he was going to use a catheter and drain her bladder. He would perform surgery when she was doing better. I asked if she would be okay, and he reassured me that she was going to be fine.

He called around ten o'clock and said that everything was fine but that he decided to keep her overnight. I had this scary feeling that she might not be okay, but he told me that she was going to be fine. I should have gone to get her because at least she would have died at home. I always thought that if she had to be put to sleep, it would be in my arms, but it didn't happen that way.

The next morning I received a phone call, and the vet said that Cookie had passed away. I screamed. I was home by myself, and I was absolutely delirious. I paged my husband because I thought I was going to kill myself.

Cookie died from uremia and hemorrhaging. I was angry because the vet had left her alone, and he had told me he was going to check on her. I didn't feel good about leaving her in the vet's office, but I did because I thought that it was for her own good.

I had never left Cookie alone before. She was always with me. I had terrible dreams that Cookie was wondering where I was and why I wasn't with her. I should have been with her. The Lord knows that if I could have done anything to save her, I would have, but I still feel guilty. I live with that guilt every day.

After Cookie Marie died, I wasn't going to let the vet dump her in the garbage. I made up my mind that I had to go the vet's office and pick up her body myself. It wasn't easy, but I had to make myself do it.

My husband and I were renting a house in Florida. We buried Cookie in the backyard at my mother's house in Florida. I remember saying to my mother that I didn't want to bury Cookie in Florida because I knew that we were going to be moving. My son dug the hole. We put her in a box and laid her to rest.

We stood at the grave and cried. I said a silent prayer. It was one of the worst days in my life. I kept her ball, toys, leash, blanket, and her little pink collar with rhinestones.

For the first few days I couldn't stand being in the house. I cried for days. My son was upset because he was close to Cookie. He loved and admired her. He would sit and watch her because she was so cute. My daughter was living in Texas when Cookie died, so she wasn't as close to her, but she loved Cookie and was upset about her death.

Two of my friends whom I met when I joined the humane society in Texas were supportive. They understood because they were animal lovers. My husband has been very support-ive. I don't know what I would have done if he hadn't been with me. I knew that he felt the same grief I did, and we were able to get through it together. I found comfort in telling every-body about Cookie. I would like everyone to have known her because she was so special.

Eight months later my mother died, and we moved back to Texas. I didn't want to go on. Life was so hard. I felt I had lost a child when I lost Cookie. I was suicidal. This may sound cold, but I didn't cry as much when my mother died as I did for Cookie. I loved my mother, but I hurt more when Cookie Marie died. Mother had been sick, so I expected her to die. I felt she was better off. I didn't expect Cookie Marie to die. People who are not pet owners don't understand.

I knew that my mother and Cookie Marie were gone, but I kept hoping I would see them again. I had to see my doctor be-cause I was so depressed. He gave me some medication that helped me a little. I didn't think that I was going to make it. I went through denial and a lot of depression. I believe that someday I will see Cookie and my mother. I have to believe that because I can't face the fact that I am never going to see them alive again.

Even after two years, I am still very depressed. Sometimes I find it hard to get up and get going. I suffer at home quietly.

I still cry at nights whenever I start thinking about her because I miss her so much. I miss her sweet personality and her companionship. I have always taken care of my animals, but Cookie was the only one that was in my heart. The fact that I haven't committed suicide proves that I must be stronger than I thought.

Throughout the years, I have lost other animals and have suffered with their loss, but nothing compared to what I experienced with Cookie Marie. I was very protective of her because she was so small. I was so careful, yet I feel that I let her down.

God gives us pets for a reason. My husband says that Cookie was given to us for a special reason. We were living in Florida because we went through some tough financial times during the Texas depression. Shortly after we built our dream home in Texas, my husband and I filed bankruptcy and had to move out. We lost almost everything, but we had Cookie.

We would have given up if it hadn't been for Cookie Marie. When my husband was depressed, she would jump up on his chair and look him in the eye and demand that he do something with her. He believes that she was here to help us, and she did. She gave me a reason to get up in the morning. We believe that she was sent by God.

On the day that Cookie died, I was so grief-stricken that I went out and bought another female Chihuahua. She was a tiny doll. I was trying to replace Cookie, but I realized that was not possible. My husband wanted to name her Cookie Marie, but I couldn't do that, so we named her Prissy Marie. She is beautiful. Prissy has a personality very similar to Cookie's. She is the boss around here and the other animals know it. I don't think I should have adopted a new pet on the same day that Cookie died, but I never wanted to be without a pet.

While you can't replace the pet that you lost, you can learn to love the new one. I took a long time to bond with Prissy Marie because I was so hurt by Cookie's death. I missed Cookie so much. Prissy is now two years old and we are doing well. Cookie Marie was here, but she is gone, and now it is Prissy's turn.

I was very lucky to have had Cookie Marie, and not a day goes by that I don't tell my husband how lucky we were. The people who abandoned Cookie Marie have no idea how happy we were to get her. It was their loss and our gain. Everybody who knew Cookie Marie loved her. I'll never get over her death.

Homer and Heidi

AS REMEMBERED BY

Sandra J. Lee

*"I believe that euthanasia is the last loving thing you can do
for your pet. People need to have the courage to let their
pets go instead of making them suffer."*

Rain or shine, Homer, my beautiful seal point Siamese
cat, loved to go on his walks every day. Every morning
he would sit in the foyer and wait impatiently to be put
in a figure-eight harness and hooked up to the leash. We would
proceed out the side door and down the driveway. When he
reached the sidewalk, he would stop, look to the left, look
ahead, and then to the right. We never knew which way he was
going to go. Depending on his mood, he would walk either one
block or two miles. When he was done for the day, he would
stop. I called it "putting on the brakes." This was my clue to
pick him up and carry him home.

Homer was smart and had a strong sense of himself. He
knew how to shake hands, roll over, retrieve, play catch, and
sit up and beg. Homer was an extraordinary cat. He was almost
like a human being.

We lived a block from Winter Park High School. The kids
thought he was the coolest cat because he walked on a leash.
Homer loved to go to the high school because he was the
center of attention there. The students would take pictures of

him walking across the campus, and for three years he was in the high school yearbook. Homer had his fifteen minutes of fame.

When we lived in Miami, Homer alerted us to an attempted burglary at our house, though we didn't realize it until the next day. He kept running into our rooms and yowling hysterically. We told him we didn't want to play tag. He ran to my mother and yowled at her, then he ran back to my room and yowled at me. Homer finally settled down after the burglar left. The next morning, we found holes in our garage door. Somebody had tried to break in.

Some years later, after we had moved to Winter Park, Homer alerted us to a malfunctioning toilet valve that was causing a flood in our house. From that point on, we took Homer's signals very seriously.

Heidi was a timid Russian blue whom we adopted. At first, Homer resented her, but they soon became great pals and grew to love each other. They loved to spend hours inspecting things and taking naps in the garage.

Heidi was a sweet, gentle little girl. She did not like strangers or company. She preferred her life to include just us. If anyone came into the house, she'd run under the bed and spend hours there before she would venture out. When she did, she kept a safe distance away.

Heidi knew when visitors were leaving. She had an uncanny ability to differentiate between someone going out the door for a moment and someone departing the premises. She would frequently stroll through the family room at the exact moment a visitor was headed down the front walk.

When Homer was almost fifteen years old, he developed chronic kidney failure. He was ill for about six weeks, during which time we took him back and forth to the vet. At the end he was so sick that we decided to have him put to sleep. We had him cremated and buried in a mass grave with other kitties at a pet cemetery.

After Homer died, Heidi visited the garage a couple of times to look for Homer. She would cry. Her voice sounded so sorrowful that it pained me. Normally she had a tiny little voice with a purr that could be felt but not heard. Her cry was a howl. After those few visits, she never went into the garage alone again.

Homer's death was difficult for my mother. She was extremely close to him. Homer loved everyone, but he was very attached to my mother. After his death, she stayed in bed and sobbed.

When Homer was alive, he would wake up my mother by purring in her ear. If that didn't work, he would climb on her nightstand, and he would whack her Baby Ben alarm clock off the nightstand. The clock would hit the bed frame and make the most horrible sound, which woke my mother up.

Seven weeks after Homer died, I was in my mother's bedroom while mom was dusting the furniture. We had been talking about Homer when suddenly the clock flew off the nightstand and hit the bed frame. We were on the other side of the room about ten or twelve feet away, and Heidi was nowhere around. There was no way that either of us had hit the clock. Ironically, I was trying to talk Mom into getting another cat, and she had said no. When the clock fell off, I said that Homer was okay—that Homer said it was all right. The incident reinforced my belief that cats have souls. It never happened again.

I believe there is a very special spot in heaven for people's animals. I got into an argument once with our former minister because he told me that animals don't have souls. I asked him, "Who died and made you God? Who decides that animals don't have souls?" If heaven doesn't have animals, then I'm not going because a heaven without animals would be my idea of hell.

After Homer passed away, we brought three new kittens into the house as company for Heidi. Introducing kittens into a house with a fourteen-and-a-half-year-old cat was a challenge, but Heidi handled it well. The kittens brought new life into her existence and, I believe, extended her life. While the kittens were bigger than Heidi, they knew she was the queen of the household and always deferred to her.

Five years after Homer died, Heidi suffered a stroke while I was at work. From the moment I walked through the door, I knew something was wrong because only the three lilac points were sitting there. Normally, the four of them were lined up in the foyer waiting for dinner. My first thought was that Heidi had died. I looked at the kittens and told them to show me where Heidi was. They yowled and ran into our front bedroom.

When Heidi had the stroke, she lost control of her bowels. The stool was fairly wet, so I don't think she had been lying there very long. She was able to pick her head up and was still very much alive. I gave her a bath and blow-dried her hair before I called the emergency clinic. It was important to me that she die with the same quiet dignity with which she had lived.

When a small animal has a stroke, nothing can be done to rehabilitate her, so I was prepared for the outcome. I was very calm. I wrapped up Heidi in her favorite towel and drove her to the clinic. She lay in my lap as I drove. I had always thought that if the cats became ill and no longer had a quality life, I would do the one last loving thing I could for them.

When I took Heidi into the clinic, the staff gave me a room to myself and told me that I could spend as much time with her as I wanted. They would come back when I was ready. I spent about ten minutes with Heidi. I sat down at her eye level and talked to her. I kept her wrapped so she wouldn't be cold. I told her how much we loved her and how much she had brought into our lives. I told her it was time for her to sleep and not to suffer anymore.

Heidi was so calm. In my heart of hearts, I believe she knew she was dying. She purred and closed her eyes. Her euthanasia was very peaceful.

I signed the paperwork to have Heidi cremated. The crematorium gave her ashes to a local garden, where the ashes were mixed into soil. Heidi helped an azalea grow at a botanical garden in Apopka. I have never visited the garden, but I am glad to know that she is living on in some form.

I was prepared for her death because I had watched her age. She was like a little old lady who was slowly but surely failing. I felt better in a way because at least she had not died while I was at work.

We kept Homer and Heidi's collars and leashes. We still have two Christmas ornaments with their likenesses. Every year to honor their memory, we put the ornaments on the tree. Sitting on our bookshelf is a lovely portrait of both Homer and Heidi. I strongly believe that you shouldn't forget about your pets just because they died.

I believe with loss there is always grief. If you consider your pets to be part of your home, then losing them is almost like losing a member of the family. You have a distinct love for them, but it's a different love than you have for your human family.

There are people whose pets are their only companions. I am very blessed to be surrounded by people who are animal lovers. I correspond with many animal lovers, particularly cat people. They can understand my grief and pain. Some people are embarrassed about grieving, but I was never embarrassed.

I cried my eyes out when we had to have Homer put to sleep. When Heidi died, I cried not so much out of sadness as out of the knowledge that I was going to miss her. With Heidi, it was like going through the phases when a person is terminally ill: you go through the emotions until you are at the point of acceptance.

If I learned anything from the loss of my pets, I learned how much dignity animals have. Both of my cats had a lot of dignity. Heidi was like a queen. She handled her aging and failing with dignity.

The most important act any pet owner can do is to put the animal ahead of personal wishes. So many people have a hard time accepting that an animal's life is coming to an end. Instead of allowing their pets to die with dignity, they make them suffer and tell themselves that their dog isn't in pain or that their cat doesn't hurt. I think that a lot of people selfishly keep their animals alive when they should love them enough to let them go. I believe that euthanasia is the last loving thing you can do for your pet. People need to have the courage to let their pets go instead of making them suffer.

Axel

AS REMEMBERED BY

Paul Bartuch

"Burying his remains was very difficult . . .
My wife and I could have filled a bucket with our tears that day."

I became involved with our K-9 program in 1987. Ours was one of the first ones in the area. Axel was a regular police officer. He had his own badge, which was round instead of five-pronged so he wouldn't get stabbed by it. When Axel died, the department gave me his badge and retired his badge number.

On the wall in our department we have pictures of all our officers who are on duty. Axel's picture was up there with everybody else's. There are laws now to protect police dogs; for example, you cannot tease or hit a police dog. The dogs are very valuable to the department.

Axel was good with kids. The police officers put on demonstrations in the local schools. We would bring the dogs in and show a short video. Depending on the ages of the kids, we would also hide narcotics. We have done narcotics searches at the high school to let students know that it would be difficult to hide anything from the dogs.

Axel once tracked a disabled child who was lost. He tracked the child two miles along the highway and lost the track at a stop light where the boy had been picked up by a couple of guys who took him to a restaurant so he could warm up. Eventually, we found the boy in the restaurant parking lot.

Axel also received commendations for tracking a couple of burglars. There were articles in several newspapers, and his picture was included.

When you work with a police dog, you learn to read your dog so you know exactly what he's doing. You learn to recognize when he's tracking a person, searching a building, or just playing a game. When he's searching for dope, I notice the subtle characteristics that somebody else may not see.

Axel's attitude changed when he worked. I noticed that his breathing and his hair changed. When Axel did a building search, I'd see him walking through the building, then all of a sudden, I'd see him prancing through the building with his head up. I would know that somebody was in there and that Axel got him.

When searching a building or looking for burglars, Axel was my eyes, my nose, and my ears, and I followed behind. It was the same when we tracked someone. He'd do the work, and I was with him as his backup. If he found the bad guy before I did and the bad guy started fighting with him, I'd have to go and protect Axel just as much as he would have protected me.

When a dog is going through a building and the person inside has a gun, the dog's going to get hit before the officer. It's scary to think that way, but that's the way the system's designed. When we train a dog, everything to him is a game. Gunshots don't bother him. When he is play-fighting or biting somebody, that's all a game. We make everything a game to him. So in a real situation everything to him is still a game unless the bad guy punches, kicks, or hurts him. Then the dog's going to get agitated.

At work, the officer and the police dog become one. You become him and he becomes you. Police dogs feel their officers' adrenaline levels going up, so their adrenaline levels go up too. Axel knew when I was upset, excited, or happy. I didn't have to say anything.

Whenever I worked, Axel worked. We were on twenty-four-hour call. We did regular patrol duties. We answered calls to check open doors, conducted building searches, tracked offenders or lost children, and conducted narcotic searches of vehicles and houses. If we had a carnival in town, Axel would be at the carnival watching the kids to make sure nothing was wrong.

When an officer gets a dog like Axel, he has to understand from the beginning that the dog is a police dog. At any time the dog could get killed. We go through training so we can learn to read our dogs and they don't get into trouble. We train our dogs to stay close to us so we're in eyesight of each other at all times. That keeps both partners alive.

A couple of times we were involved in fights where Axel had to come out of the car. One incident began with an officer answering a call at 11 P.M. It was time for a shift change, and our officers were headed back to the department. The responding officer walked in on a fight between a motorcycle gang and some other people in an apartment complex. He called for help. I was the closest one on the street, so I headed there and called for more backup.

By the time I arrived, there were about fifty people with baseball bats and knives. The first officer was in the middle of it. Axel and I climbed out of our car. Axel started barking. He snapped at a few people and bit a few. If it hadn't been for him, we never would have been able to split up that fight. Axel held a riot situation down to nothing because the people were afraid of him.

There was a funny incident involving Axel and another officer during a building-search practice. The officer was wearing a full-body bite suit, which was big and heavy. He looked like the Michelin Tire character. He put the suit on in a bathroom, which was his hiding place. Axel was supposed to find him and bark to alert me. The officer was to let Axel bite him on the arm.

Axel barked like crazy when he found him. The officer swung the door open and got stuck in the doorway due to the bulky suit. With both the officer's arms stuck, the only thing left for Axel to bite was the man's groin. The officer was lucky that he had the pads on. By the time I arrived, the guy was yelling. I knew he got bit through the suit because the pitch of his voice was very high. The rest of us were on the floor laughing. I barely got Axel off of him because I was laughing so hard.

Toward the end of his life, Axel became lethargic and slow. He wasn't eating. At first, I thought it was because of the hot weather. Usually he was very active and playful and never slowed down. He was ball crazy. Axel loved to play. I knew there was a problem when he stopped chasing the ball around.

Our vet told us to take him to some specialists at Purdue University. They diagnosed cancer in his spleen, his lungs, and throughout his body. They said that it would be painful to put Axel through an operation, and they gave him only a 2 percent chance of making it through the surgery, which was only to take out part of the cancer of the spleen. They gave him only a couple of months to live.

The specialists figured it would be better to put him down than to have him go through that pain and agony. Whether for a pet or a police dog, euthanasia is a very difficult decision to make. You have to think of the welfare of the dog, and you have to think of the family. If you've ever seen a person die of cancer, you know the pain he goes through. I couldn't see Axel going through that pain. And I couldn't see myself and the family having to go through it, especially since we have two young children. It was better that we did it the way we did.

As far as the kids knew, Axel passed away on his own. The kids were only seven and eight years old. We did not explain to them how we had to put Axel down. I don't think that they would have understood at that age. They knew he was very sick, and they had seen their great-grandmother die of cancer, so they had an idea.

We picked a day to put him down that was only seven days from the time we received the news that he had cancer. He was having a hard time walking—his back end wasn't working right. We tried to keep him to see how he would do, but he was very weak.

When we made the decision to put him down, the vet's office was fantastic. We had Axel cremated. The pet cemetery knew he was a police officer, so the staff took care of everything. He was put in a urn that could be buried in the ground. They made a plaque with his picture on it.

Axel is buried in the backyard at my house. Burying his remains was very difficult. My wife and I talked about the things that we did together with Axel, and it hit me that he wasn't coming back. My wife and I could have filled a bucket with our tears that day. We felt Axel was in heaven. When we buried Axel, we didn't have the kids present. They saw the grave after they came home from school.

We have a female Rottweiler who grew up with Axel. She would look around the yard for him. She'd go in his kennel and look in the doghouse. It took a while for her to understand that he was gone.

I have Axel's choker collar and his ball. I didn't get rid of anything. We have some pictures of him from when we were on the job. I also have a scrapbook with photos and articles of the different things we did.

His death was a big shock to everybody—to the department and to the village. The people may not have felt the same way as I did about Axel, but in some way they felt the loss because Axel used to do a lot of things around the town. Everybody gave their condolences, and I received a lot of cards.

People who own businesses regretted the loss of Axel because of the building searches and the security that he gave them. People called and wanted to know when the next dog was coming. I think the kids missed him the most because he was fantastic with them.

Losing a dog like Axel was like losing a part of myself. A pet can live with you for so many years that he becomes a part of the family. I was with Axel so much that he became more than a part of my family.

Losing a police dog is very difficult because when I go out to the squad car, there isn't a dog there anymore. I am alone again. Axel was the partner I used to talk to and play with. Suddenly, he's not there. The loss creates a very lonely and empty feeling. I answer calls where I could use him, and he's not there.

When a K-9 officer loses his dog, he should get another dog quickly. That way the officer can get back into the routine. You never lose the memories, and you can never compare. There was only one Axel, and there's only going to be one new dog.

Other people may compare and say that this one looked prettier, this one looked nicer, or this one looked bigger. As an officer, I can't do a search and say, "Oh, Axel could have done it better." I won't do that. I taught Axel the work he did, so if I taught Axel, I can also teach the new dog.

I didn't talk about Axel's death with a lot of people except for my family and other K-9 officers. We have our own group who have trained together every other Tuesday for years. Besides training together, we hang out together. Our families even get together. We're very close.

A few officers in the group had lost dogs before, so they were people with whom I could talk. They knew how I felt. It was very emotional. Guys cried. Every K-9 officer who knew about Axel's death cried because they have dogs. Each of the officers knows that one day everybody's going to go through the same thing.

I have been using a different squad car since Axel died because mine was only set up for K-9 duty. My car won't be used until a new dog comes in. We are also changing the car. I asked the department to take Axel's name off the car because it would remind me about how I had to put him down.

I'm ready to go on with a new dog. I'm not giving up on the old one, but I'm ready to move ahead. Axel is on my mind, and he will never be forgotten. Axel is outside in the backyard. Anytime I want to go outside and talk to him, he is there.

Smoky and Snorkel

AS REMEMBERED BY

Gary Ellis Fryfogle

"Time has a tendency to heal the wounds—you never forget the loss, but it becomes a little easier to talk about."

In France during the seventeenth century, the fire pumpers were pulled by teams of horses. Dalmatians were used as coach dogs. They kept the horses calm in the stables. Even when the fire service became mechanized, people in this country still associated Dalmatians with fire departments. The dairy business, which also required horses to pull carts, didn't use Dalmatians. The fire service used Dalmatians because it had so many horses.

The personnel in the fire department has changed dramatically over the years. When I came into the fire department, a mascot was a public relations tool, and the general public expected to see a fire dog when they came to the station for a tour. Over the years, the newer guys felt that having a dog around the station was a chore—having to let the dog in and out and having to clean up the dog hair. About half of the department was in favor of having a mascot, and for the other half it was a pain in the posterior.

Smoky and Snorkel played more of an image role than anything else. We tried early on to take Smoky on fire calls, but it didn't work out because of all the activity that goes on at a fire—

guys running around grabbing hoses or grabbing another tool off the truck. Smoky thought it was a game and would run around barking.

Smoky was relegated to being at the station for the kids to play with whenever they came for a tour. When the kids came in, the first question they would ask was, "Where's the fire doggie?"

The community was aware of the animals. In fact, when Smoky was replaced, we had a contest to name the new fire dog. We provided a $100 savings bond to the winner, who was a twelve-year-old boy. The members of the fire department voted on the winner.

Smoky and Snorkel were pedigreed dogs. Smoky was given to us by a family in the community who raised Dalmatians. Snorkel was purchased at the county fair in Wellington, Ohio, by our mayor, who donated Snorkel to the department.

The dogs lived at the station; they were trained to remain on the grounds, so they didn't have to be chained up. They were housebroken. When they wanted to go to the bathroom, they would either stand at the door or bark.

The fire dog mascots became a liability issue. We would put Snorkel in a room during the tours, especially when pre-schoolers came. Whenever the children saw the dog, they would run up to him and grab him. Snorkel didn't know what was going on.

Animals are perceptive, and they can tell whether a person loves them or simply tolerates them. Ever since I was a little kid, I have had dogs. I have played with them, hugged them, and kissed them. My dogs were an important part of my life.

Smoky and Snorkel were probably closer to me than to anyone else in the department. One day when I was off duty, I stopped by the station with one of the firefighters, and Smoky came out to greet us. The other firefighter and I played with her in the front yard, then we put Smoky in the car and went to one of the local bars. The bartender knew all the guys in the department. The other firefighter and I had a beer, and we had the bartender cook up a hamburger for Smoky. Everybody in the bar was having a grand old time, and nobody objected. Smoky sat there while we fed her the hamburger and we finished our beer. Then we took her back to the department.

Snorkel liked different kinds of food. He loved to eat pizza, steak sandwiches, and McDonald's hamburgers. On hot days Snorkel would catch a whiff of the hamburgers cooking at a nearby McDonald's, and he'd violate the rule of not leaving the building. There was an access driveway that led to the back of McDonald's. Snorkel would go down the driveway and proceed to have himself a picnic at McDonald's.

One evening the guys let Snorkel go outside for a while. They were watching television and forgot about Snorkel. A couple hours later it dawned on them that Snorkel hadn't come back. They looked for him but couldn't find him. They were worried because the chief would have had a fit if anything had happened to Snorkel. The police pulled up with Snorkel in the back of the cruiser. They brought him in and told us that they had found Snorkel at the local pizza place. He had pizza sauce all over his face.

Both Smoky and Snorkel had to be euthanized. Smoky had a liver disorder and hepatitis. She was euthanized in 1979. A couple of the guys were handy with carpentry, so they made her a little casket. After she was euthanized, we brought her back and wrapped her up in one of the blankets that she used. We dug an area where she loved to sunbathe and made up a little headstone with her name and the years that she spent in the department.

Snorkel developed spinal arthritis. He was on cortisone for a while, but his condition progressed into the cervical area around his neck. There wasn't anything the vet could do for him. The neck area became very sensitive. I am a paramedic, so I understood the medical aspects of his condition. I thought I could extend Snorkle's life with an exercise program and a lot of love. His mobility and flexibility improved, but when the arthritis reached the cervical area, it became irreversible.

I kept Snorkel at my house during the last three months of his illness. I walked him as much as possible. He ate like a king. My wife worked for a country club, so he was eating steak and prime rib leftovers.

The decision to put Snorkel to sleep in 1992 was not easy. Unfortunately, there was no way of reversing the spinal arthritis. I was devastated, but the decision stopped his suffering.

His death was difficult for me because Snorkel was a big part of my life. He was like a member of the family. I shed quite a few tears over Snorkel's death. When people say that big boys don't cry, that is a lot of baloney. We do cry, especially when we lose someone near and dear to us. Time has a tendency to heal the wounds—you never forget the loss, but it becomes a little easier to talk about.

When I received Snorkel's ashes, I spread them on some of his favorite areas. I got a little misty while I was doing it. His ashes were all over the place because he didn't have one specific place that he liked.

The beauty of animals is their gift of unconditional love. I can discipline them one minute, and the next minute they're kissing me on the face. When I come home, they are wagging their tails and are happy to see me.

The best advice I could give anybody is to love their pets and enjoy them while they have them. Someday they might be making the decision to put them to sleep, so they should make every minute count.

I would like the community to remember that Smoky and Snorkel did an outstanding job. They served their community and did their duty.

Felicia

AS REMEMBERED BY

Sally Brown

*"At times I feel like I have accepted her death, and
at other times I don't. It helps to talk about her."*

My mother always said that I should have been a vet
because I love animals so much. I have a great rapport
with them. I feel that I can relate more to animals than
I can to some people I know. If I had my way, I would have a
house full of animals. I believe that animals are the only friends
I would ever need.

Pets give unconditional love. I can walk around the house
and look horrible, but they don't care. I can yell at them and
they still love me. It's that unconditional love that I can't receive
from people. Many people hold grudges and are not willing to
understand others because their love is not unconditional.

Throughout my life, I have found homeless animals and have
taken them home. I found Felicia underneath a cart by a grocery store. I couldn't leave her because I was afraid she would
get hit by a car, so I took her home. I believe she was about six
weeks old when I found her because she was walking, her eyes
were open, and she could eat.

Felicia was a unique cat. Her eyes would change colors from
green to yellow to blue. I had never seen a cat with eyes that
did that. She had long hair that was mostly white and brown

with a tiger stripe, and her stomach and paws were white. Felicia was a gorgeous cat.

Even when Felicia was a little kitten, she had her own personality. She loved to lie on my stomach and knead my stomach with her little paws. It didn't hurt because I had her declawed. It was our special time together.

Felicia loved to antagonize my two dogs, Tosha and Tai. She would look at them to make sure that they saw her, and when they did, they would chase her. During the first part of the chase, it was a cat followed by two dogs, but coming back it would be a dog, a cat, and a dog. It was a game, and she seemed to have fun.

Felicia was like my daughter. I treat all my animals like they are my kids. I believe that if I treat my pets with respect, I will get respect, and they will do what I ask. I talked to Felicia and my dogs as if they were humans.

Felicia never did anything to make me mad. She was a docile cat. Felicia may have hissed at my other two cats occasionally, but she would end up taking care of them and cleaning them. They would sleep and play together.

My dogs loved to go outside and play with snow, but I never let Felicia go out and experience the snow. Felicia loved looking out the windows. She would hop on the couch or on the television and look outside.

Our quality time was at night when she jumped up on my bed and climbed on my stomach. She would lie there for a while and then get up and move to the corner of the bed, where she would stay until I fell asleep.

Felicia was my baby. When I would leave to go to work, it sounded like she was calling "Mom." In the middle of the night, she would run through the house looking for me. I would hear her and call her. Then she would run and jump onto the bed. She would take her spot on the little pillow I had for her. She liked to be wherever I was.

Felicia had her special spots around the house where she loved to lie down. One spot was in front of the fireplace. She looked like a statue in front of the fireplace, like she belonged there.

Felicia never had any special toys, but she did have a passion for paper bags and boxes. If the bags were standing up, she jumped in them. At Christmastime she would climb in the gift boxes to see what was in them.

I had Felicia for about nine years and was in shock when she died because her death was so unexpected. On the day she became sick, I knew that something was wrong, but I thought she had a fur ball that she couldn't get out. She was always getting fur balls and throwing up. The next morning her body was cold, so I called the vet.

Felicia hated to ride in the car, and when I took her to the vet's, she howled because she was so scared. My son, Josh, held her and tried to comfort her, even though he is allergic to cats. He loved Felicia and would let her do anything. She sometimes licked his hair as if she was cleaning him.

The vet took her temperature, and it didn't even register on the thermometer. I told him to do what he had to do, that I didn't care what it cost.

As I was leaving her at the animal hospital for some tests, I gave her a kiss, and I told her that I loved her. I also gave her my pink rabbit's foot from my key chain because she loved to play with it. I asked the staff to hook the rabbit's foot on her cage where she could see it.

I called about 1:30 P.M. to check on her, and the staff were still giving her an IV, so they asked me to call back about two o'clock. I called back and asked if I could check on her, but they were going to do a chest x-rays, so they asked me to come at 5:30 P.M.

When I arrived, Felicia was quiet and looked bad. I cried and called out "Fee Fee," one of her nicknames, and she howled. She sounded like she was in pain. She was breathing funny. I knew that she wasn't coming back home, and it hurt to see her in pain. I did a lot of praying while she was in the hospital.

I was glad that I went to visit her because I knew she wouldn't make it through the night. I wanted to believe that she was going to be okay, but her body was cold. I knew in my heart that she was going to die.

The next morning around eight o'clock, the vet's office called and left a message on my telephone. When I returned home around 9:30 A.M., I called the office and talked to the vet. I knew Felicia was dead and started to cry.

Dr. Mowery felt bad because he still didn't know exactly what was wrong with her and how he should have treated her condition. He asked me if I wanted him to do an autopsy. I said that he should because I wanted to know why she died.

Even though Felicia wasn't a good candidate for surgery, Dr. Mowery wondered whether she would have survived if we had taken the chance. I told him that there was no way that she would have. I could tell that Dr. Mowery felt bad because he couldn't help Felicia.

I was fine until I arrived at the vet's office in the afternoon. The staff gave back my rabbit's foot and a plastic object that had been found in her intestine.

Dr. Mowery thought that the object may have contributed to her condition, but it shouldn't have killed her because the area around her intestine wasn't swollen or discolored. He didn't know what killed her. She had fluid in her chest cavity, and her lungs were floating in it. They had pushed 350 milliliters of fluid through the IV, and her bladder did not have anything in it.

I cried all the way home. It was so bizarre how she died. I couldn't believe it. I was in shock. I felt guilty and kept thinking that if I was a vet maybe I would have picked up on it, but I'm not a vet, and I did the best I could. I try not to think of the time when Felicia was suffering.

When I took her to the vet's, I knew that she wasn't coming back. I kept telling myself that she was, but I knew better. Her body deteriorated so fast. I felt bad that I had to leave her because I knew that nobody would be there with her. What bothered me the most was that she had to pass away by herself. I wanted my Felicia back.

I was upset that I had allowed her to die. I should have noticed something was wrong, and I was bothered that I hadn't. I was very apologetic after she died. I kept saying, "I am so sorry, Felicia." I never meant for her to go like that. I expected her to live at least another six years. She had never once been sick, and I kept her inside the house.

I wanted to get another kitten the same day that Felicia died, but I felt guilty because I thought I should grieve a little more. I thought that Felicia would think, How can you do this? I haven't even been gone twenty-four hours. I know that I will never find another cat like her. Felicia was so special and unique.

At times I feel like I have accepted her death, and at other times I don't. It helps to talk about her. The saddest time for me comes late at night because she would sleep with me. Sometimes my brain does not want to shut off. I worry about her and I miss her. I decided to keep her ashes and will probably have them buried with me when I die. I will get a pretty urn for her ashes. I loved her so much. She was so much a part of my life.

I took the loss of my cat harder than the death of my mom. Mom died of cancer. I knew she was hurting and that she was in a lot of pain, so I was at peace when she died because she wasn't suffering anymore.

My mom lived in Indiana, and I lived in Ohio, so I saw her as much as I could. I called her every day. I spent my thirtieth birthday with her, and one week later she died. I knew what the outcome was going to be, so I prepared myself for her death. When she died, I knew she was in a better place. I was more prepared for her death than I was for Felicia's. Felicia's death was a shock because it was unexpected.

I believe that cats have souls like humans. I'm certain that my mom is taking care of Felicia. I truly believe that.

Animals are a part of my life. I don't want to go through the pain again, but I can't live without animals because I love them—especially cats. They are very smart. Cats have their own personalities. Felicia and I had a great rapport. I could look at Felicia and tell what she wanted.

Having my dogs, Tosha and Tai, helped me get through Felicia's death. I still have her cat litter box. I had just gone to the grocery store when she died, so I had tons of cat food. I cleaned the litter box in case I adopted another kitten. I even have Felicia's fur from when I combed her over the weekend. I couldn't bring myself to throw it away. I kept the pink rabbit's foot on my key chain, and it goes everywhere with me.

Some people understand my grief to a degree, but nobody could really know unless she loves animals as much as I do. The people who know me are aware of how much I love my animals, so they have been very sympathetic and caring. They know that it was like losing a child. Some of them tried to get me another cat, but I said that I was not ready.

Some people don't understand how I feel about animals and will look at me like I'm crazy. But this is the way I was born. I love animals.

One of the reasons I don't go to the humane society is because I want to take all the animals home. If I ever win the lottery, I am going to have a farm with a big old barn converted with central air and heat, and I will take every animal I can find at the humane society.

Several months after Felicia passed away, I adopted two kittens. Their names are KC and Kisha, and they are very cute. Kisha is white and has perfect gray and beige circles on her back. She is very pretty. KC will have long fur like Felicia, and she has a lot of Felicia's personality. The kittens are a laugh a minute.

Felicia's ashes are still resting on the end table by my bed. I took ceramic lessons two years ago and made a cat statue of Felicia. The statue sits in front of the fireplace because Felicia was so much a part of that scenery. Every time I look at the statue, it reminds me of her.

I have a picture of Felicia lying on her back, and I am going to have it enlarged. Then I am going to encase all her belongings. I have shared my story of Felicia so that she will live forever.

Monty

AS REMEMBERED BY

Rita Starr

*"The most significant thing I did was to let myself cry for hours—
just cry and cry. It was so healing that once I had cried all those tears,
I was fine. . . . I had accepted her death."*

Monty was a gift from my ex-husband. We were dating at the time and I was living in an apartment. My hamster had died, so he bought me a dog for my birthday. I was nineteen years old.

Monty helped alleviate some of the loneliness of college and being away from home. The best thing about Monty was sleeping with her. She had a strong personality and always created lots of action.

Our relationship was like mother and daughter. Her constant yapping drove me nuts and sometimes made me angry. But what I valued so much was that she was always available for love. Monty was a positive source of love.

When Monty was eleven years old, she began losing her eyesight. One day I had let her outside to go to the bathroom. Even though we lived on a busy street, I didn't worry since she usually went out and came right back in. This time she was hit by a car. Although there wasn't a mark on her, she still died.

She was lying next to the side of the road when I saw her. My heart dropped. Her long hair was blowing in the wind. She looked like a beautiful fur ball. I picked her up in a blanket and brought her inside.

My eight-year-old son was on his way to school when Monty was hit by the car. I made the mistake of insisting that he still go to school. I wish I had kept him home with me since he had grown up with Monty.

Initially, I blamed others. I was angry at my son. I was less sensitive to his needs because I was in so much pain. I was overwhelmed with feelings, but I don't think I verbalized my feelings to him. Later, my son and I talked about Monty and cried together.

We buried Monty in my mother's rose garden. My mother helped me uproot one of her pink rose bushes. She was also very attached to Monty.

I spent the rest of the day grieving. The most significant thing I did was to let myself cry for hours—just cry and cry. I cried for about five hours straight. It was so healing that once I had cried all those tears, I was fine. I didn't go through a depression because I allowed myself to grieve and cry. I had accepted her death by the end of the day. After I had cried, I re-alized how useful it would have been for my son to have stayed home and cried.

My mother was instrumental in my healing. She never made me feel inadequate for crying. She wept too. Monty was like my first child. I allowed myself to empty my heart of tears. I told stories of what I appreciated about Monty and what I missed.

I didn't share the loss with my friends. I don't think that most people understand grieving, and they probably would have thought that I was crazy for crying so hard for my pet.

I learned the value of allowing yourself to grieve—to fully grieve for the loss. You can accept anything if you allow your-self to go through the natural grieving process and not rush it. What was interesting was that I hardly felt any sadness after the day we buried Monty.

I think people can get through anything if they allow themselves to express their feelings with tears. My personal experience with Monty's loss was so empowering—to know what it feels like to be so deeply attached to someone and to be able to grieve and let it go almost completely. Regardless of the way people have been hurt, they can heal, recover, and reclaim their original aliveness.

I think that it is possible to recover from all painful experiences. If you sort through the experience and put it in context of the innocence that you had in the relationship, you will find great wisdom in the experience.

Unfortunately, most of us are forced to remain quiet by the cultural values surrounding feelings. Many people think we should keep our feelings to ourselves. We don't get to talk and to process what has happened to us. I think that keeps us wounded.

One of my sons died when he was three months old. He was in the hospital for two months because he was premature. He was home for only a month. I felt guilty and didn't allow myself to grieve. I didn't talk about it and took tranquilizers to stop crying. Consequently, I postponed a heavy depression for over a year.

Since I postponed grieving over my son's death, I had a strong desire to replace him immediately. With Monty, I didn't rush to replace her. I didn't own another animal for several years. I had felt complete with Monty. I didn't have to replace the emptiness because the emptiness wasn't there. I had grieved immediately with Monty, but I didn't allow myself to grieve for my son. The people around me were in so much pain that they didn't allow me to do grieve for him either.

I experienced a loss in my early childhood that left me frightened of owning another pet for many years. When I was three years old, my father brought home some white rabbits. From his point of view, he wanted fatten them up and then eat them. From my point of view, they were my darlings. My father said that he had to kill them because we were becoming too attached to them. The experience taught me to believe that if we love something, it will die.

My mother had to cook the rabbits for my father, but she couldn't eat them because she kept seeing their little pink eyes. They were all on a plate in the middle of the table. You can imagine what this did to a three year old to have her friends cut up and placed on the table in front of her.

Our culture expects people to be over a death as soon as the funeral is over rather than taking the time that is needed to grieve. Some think that if people stop crying, then the hurting stops, but actually they are forced to prolong the grief.

Laughter is one of the natural processes that begins after the grieving. Once people have grieved enough, then they can think back and begin to laugh. Laughter is very healing.

Human beings naturally have an inner strength. But when we get wounded, we lose connection to that strength. When we heal the wound, we are reconnected with the power.

My advice to others is to take the time to grieve. Find an environment where you can feel safe and don't have to worry about being criticized by people. If you can find someone who honors and values the grieving process and who will spend an hour or two with you, that is even better; but you can do it yourself. Set some time aside and cry your eyes out—be dramatic. Let the tears gush. Look at the pictures of your pet and remember the most painful memories and talk out loud about them. Talk about how much you are going to miss her and how much you loved her.

There is a bottom to grief. It is not as endless as it may feel. Toward the end of the crying process, you might find yourself yawning. Let those deep yawns come. This is part of a natural healing process. All you have to do is use it. You can grieve through your loss and move on. Go with the flow.

Snuggle and Sandy Jo

AS REMEMBERED BY

Dawn Henrichs

"I feel connected to them at their graves. . . .
I feel close to them there."

When I was in grade school, I would bring stray dogs to our home. One time I brought home a collie. My dad wouldn't let me keep him, so we found him a home. I was sad because I had always wanted a collie like Lassie.

When my dad finally agreed to let me have a dog, we found an ad in the newspaper for a Border collie. We could tell that she was part Labrador, but I didn't care. She was the pup of the litter that no one wanted. On our way home, the puppy snuggled close to me and laid her head on my shoulder. My mom thought we should call her Snuggle. I fell in love with her.

I was only eight years old when we adopted Snuggle, and it was the happiest day of my life. She was one of the best things to ever happen to me. Snuggle was my best friend. We grew up together. She was there for me when no one else was. She would sit and listen to me ramble on for hours. When I was down, she would lick my face and try to cheer me up.

Sometimes she would get her ball and drop it at my feet. I still remember the first time when she tried to play ball with me. I was outside bouncing a basketball, and she came up from behind me and took it. That's when we started playing ball together.

She also loved to play Frisbee. She could jump up in the air and catch the Frisbee, but she kept tearing up the Frisbees.

Snuggle loved to chase cars. She could see the road from her pen, so she would anxiously pace back and forth. Even when there was nothing coming, she would still run. She would become hot from running, but she wouldn't stop.

Snuggle was like a kid. She was a great dog, and I loved her with all my heart. Whatever food we had, Snugs would eat it.

When I first adopted Snuggle, I never thought that I would have to say goodbye to her. Snug was about eight weeks old when I adopted her, and she was twelve years old when she was diagnosed with bone cancer. I was crushed when the vet said there was nothing he could do for her. I never felt so helpless in my life.

I had such a strong bond with Snugs that I couldn't put her to sleep. I didn't want to let her go. I hoped that some miracle would happen, and she would get well again. I wouldn't have been able to live with myself if I had ended her life while she still had a chance to get well.

In reality, Snug's condition was terminal. Snugs was dying and I couldn't face it. She was diagnosed in November of 1992, and I finally said goodbye to her on February 20, 1993.

Snuggle's health declined rapidly. She was in obvious pain, and I hated seeing her that way. I finally decided to have her euthanized, but it was not because I wanted my pain to be over. Her death was just the beginning of my grieving. It was the hardest period I've ever been through in my life.

I will never forget that last day with Snuggle. I held her on my lap all the way to the vet's office. She wanted to chase cars, but I wouldn't let her. Snug soon grew weak and tired, so she laid her head on my shoulder. I whispered in her ear, "I love you, Snuggle." And she looked at me like, I love you too,

Dawn. Then she lay down on my lap and hung her head over my arm. She lay close to me as if she knew that it would be the last time we would be together. When we arrived, the nurse asked me if I wanted to witness the process, and I shook my head no. She left us alone in the room for a few minutes and came back in to have me sign the release papers that gave the vet permission to do the euthanasia. She asked if I was ready for the assistants to come in and get Snuggle, and I nodded. I couldn't talk because I was bawling so hard.

Two assistants came in, and Snuggle looked straight into my eyes as they took her away. I will never forget that look. It was as if she was trying to say goodbye but at the same time she was saying, Where are they taking me, Dawn? Don't let them take me. I lost control there and then. That was the last time I saw Snugs. I cried all the way home.

I put Snug to sleep because she was suffering. I thought it was in her best interest to die without pain and to die with dignity. I couldn't ask her to die in agony for me. I loved her too much.

When Snuggle died, so did a part of me. I didn't want to let her go, and I didn't want to say goodbye. I cried for days. I felt guilty because I felt I had killed her. I thought other people would look down on me for killing her.

People who don't own pets have no possible way of knowing how bad it tears you up inside when you euthanize your pet. I took it day by day, and I tried to avoid people who thought that I was stupid and silly to grieve over a pet. I took Snug's death hard because she was the first pet that belonged to me. I missed her a lot.

My mother's dog, Jag, got along well with Snuggle. He missed Snuggle too. He would go to Snug's pen and would look to see if she was there. I would say, "She's not there, Jag."

My mother took it hard because she also liked Snuggle. It was hard for her to let Snuggle go.

I lost my grandpa six days after I lost Snuggle. My grandpa died of a heart attack at his home. I took my grandpa's death very hard. I cried a lot. I was brokenhearted and devastated. I hit an all-time low—I felt lost and didn't know where to turn. I would go out to Snug's pen and sit on her doghouse and talk to her. I felt close to her when I did that.

I used my grandpa's funeral as a way to say goodbye to Snug. It helped a lot. I kept Snuggle's toys and her collar to feel closer to her.

The only thing that kept me going was knowing that I still had Sandy Jo. She had been abused as a puppy, and my brother's friend had rescued her. When he moved, he couldn't take Sandy Jo with him, so he sought a good home for her. My brother suggested that I take her. We had to convince my dad to let me have her. When I adopted Sandy Jo, she was four years old, and I had her for eight years.

Sandy Jo was a registered Shetland sheepdog. She was scared when she came to our house, but she soon learned that I wasn't going to hurt her. I never once laid a hand on her. I simply controlled her with my voice.

Sandy Jo was extremely protective of me. One time she bit a friend because he hit me. We were playing around and hitting each other in fun, but Sandy Jo didn't like that. She would not let anyone touch me.

She didn't like to play with toys; instead, she loved to follow me around. Everywhere I went, there was Sandy Jo. She loved to bark excessively. She would even bark at my dad when he came home. We knew that she was sick when she stopped barking at my dad.

When Sandy became ill, I took her to the vet and he ran some tests. The vet came back into the room without Sandy Jo. I knew that something was seriously wrong. He told me that Sandy Jo was suffering from kidney failure. It couldn't be cured or reversed. He proceeded to tell us that if she was human, she would need a kidney transplant as soon as possible. Sandy Jo also had a heart murmur, and her liver was starting to fail. The vet gave her only two to six months to live—a year at the absolute most.

Once again, I felt extremely helpless. There was nothing I could do except let her go. I couldn't bear to see her suffer, so I had her put to sleep. It hadn't even been a year since Snuggle died. I felt so abandoned and alone.

The nights were the hardest for me because Sandy Jo used to sleep on the floor beside my bed. She used to follow me around the house, and suddenly she wasn't there anymore.

I have had a hard time adjusting to being without either Snuggle or Sandy Jo. I don't think I will ever fully adjust because they will always be a part of my life. I went through all the phases of grieving—the shock, denial, anger, depression, guilt, and acceptance.

I isolated myself after my dogs died—being by myself and letting it all out helped me. I didn't like talking about my loss. Depression and guilt lasted the longest. I cried a lot. I spent a lot of time in my room by myself. I skipped a couple of weeks of college after Snuggle and Sandy Jo died because it was hard to concentrate. I didn't eat for a few days because I lost my appetite.

Snuggle and Sandy Jo meant the world to me. I loved them with all my heart and still do. I will always visit their graves and put flowers on the graves. I think about them often, and I still cry. I don't think that I have fully accepted their deaths, but I've gotten better because now I can think about the good times, and I'm able to smile and laugh. Not a day goes by that I don't miss my dogs.

Some of my friends were very supportive, but others I wanted to slap. I stayed away from people who didn't understand. My father understood. He was the one who told me to adopt my new dog, Shadow, so I wouldn't be alone.

I experienced some hallucinations after Sandy Jo died. I felt that Sandy Jo's spirit had come to visit me. I don't believe that her spirit actually came to visit me, but it seemed so real. One day shortly after Sandy Jo died, I felt her presence in my room. Her presence did not stay long. I felt her nuzzling gently against my leg with her nose like she always did to get my attention.

It scared me because I thought that I was going nuts. I told myself that I was hallucinating. That made me feel better. That was the only time she touched me.

I could feel Sandy Jo's presence intuitively. Though I couldn't physically feel her or see her, I spoke to her. I told her that I was sorry because I didn't see her before the vet euthanized her and I didn't say goodbye. I also told her that I loved her and to find Snug so they could take good care of each other. Then she left and hasn't been back.

I was never visited by Snug's spirit, and I believe that Sandy Jo's presence was a hallucination. I had a lot of mixed feelings at that time, and I believe that it was my mind playing out those feelings. I felt a lot of sadness and guilt. I felt helpless because I didn't have either of my dogs to lean on. I felt that nobody understood what I was going through, and I felt empty inside.

I find it strange that the only place I feel connected to them is at their graves. For some reason, I feel close to them there.

I had a tough struggle, but I feel that I have accepted the deaths of my dogs. I have kept their collars, tags, and pictures for memories. I read the book *The Loss of a Pet* by Wallace Sife. It helped me realize that I wasn't alone and that what I was feeling was normal.

I would advise people who have lost a pet to allow another pet to enter their hearts. But don't get another pet until you are ready. If you get another pet too soon, you will resent it, and that will not be fair to the new pet. Only you will know when you are ready. When you are ready, remember that the new pet will not replace the one that died. It will still give you unconditional love, joy, and companionship. It will help ease your pain and help you to move on.

Shadow is a black Lab/Chesapeake Bay retriever mix. I didn't get Shadow until I was ready. I have had to adjust to puppyhood again, and I didn't realize how much time and patience it takes to raise a puppy. I got Shadow at the local humane society when she was eight weeks old. Having her helped lessen the pain and loneliness. Shadow will not replace Snuggle and Sandy Jo because they can never be replaced.

Shadow follows me everywhere. She loves going on car rides. Shadow will tear up the house when she is left alone for a long time. She is my best friend, and I spoil her rotten because I love her.

Snuggle and Sandy Jo gave me friendship, love, and joy. I have their photographs on my mirror, so I can see them every morning. It's easy to see how much they meant to me and how I honor them for their part in my life. Snuggle and Sandy Jo were such joys.

Sugar

AS REMEMBERED BY

Christi Warren

*"I do not feel guilty for putting Sugar to sleep because I know
I tried everything humanly possible to save him."*

The second I saw Sugar I loved him. We had gone to a breeder because I wanted a black cat. Sugar attached himself to me. He crawled all over me and purred. He sat on my lap. If I stood up, he followed me. I decided to buy him instead of a black cat. He was about twelve weeks old. I had him for only eighteen months.

Sugar and I were inseparable. I used to tell my husband that I was having an affair with Sugar. If I said Sugar's name, he was right there. He was fun, playful, and very well behaved. As soon as I came home from work, he came out and jumped on my lap. Sugar was a wonderful animal.

When we had had Sugar for ten months, we took him to a veterinarian because he had a cold. I never thought in a million years that the vet was going to tell us that we had a major problem, that Sugar was very sick.

Sugar was diagnosed with feline infectious peritonitis (FIP), which is a virus that attacks the internal organs. It affects predominantly the respiratory and neurological systems. There are two forms of FIP: a wet form and a dry form. Sugar had the dry form. It is an immune deficiency problem. The veterinarian wanted us to put Sugar to sleep, but we were able to keep him alive for eight more months.

We had visited a traditional veterinarian who wanted to put Sugar on steroids and medications that would suppress the symptoms but would not cure him. I decided that I did not want to lose this cat. I was not going to accept that Sugar was doomed, so I read various books on feline illnesses and found out about the possibility of consulting a holistic veterinarian.

I called the publishers of one book. They referred me to a woman up north and she referred me to a man in North Carolina. I had phone consultations with him. He never met Sugar in person, but I was able to describe Sugar's symptoms, and he was able to tell me what to do.

I made Sugar's food from scratch. I bought lamb or calves' livers and cooked them in a special way. I bought brown rice and shredded vegetables. I added vitamins such as vitamin C. I bought the items that the doctor in North Carolina suggested. We used different remedies for pain and discomfort so we wouldn't have to drug Sugar. The vet often made homemade remedies for Sugar and shipped them overnight to me. I didn't do anything except go to work and come home to take care of Sugar, which was like a full-time job itself. I would even come home for lunch in order to take care of him.

I did not want him to be in the hospital, so a local veterinarian taught me how to administer an IV drip, which I did two times a day. Sugar weighed only four pounds because he wasn't eating.

Sugar slept with us every night. He jumped on the bed when we climbed into bed. He would sleep on my stomach or on the edge of the bed. Near the end, he stopped doing that. He also wouldn't let me hold him, which was a sign that he was very uncomfortable.

The last day before we finally decided that we were going to put him to sleep, he had gone into the walk-in closet and didn't want to come out. I brought food in for him, and I made a bed for myself in the closet so I could sleep with him and make sure he was okay. I knew there was no way I could keep Sugar alive after that night because he could not walk anymore. When he tried to walk, he fell down. His balance was off. He was in pain. He was having a hard time breathing.

My husband and I took Sugar in to see the vet, who said that there was no way Sugar was going to make it. We could keep him alive, but he would be miserable. The vet was understanding. We took Sugar home, but we decided that the next morning we would have him put to sleep. We were both sad.

The doctor said that we could come in at any time. Our vet was like a family member. We talked to him practically every day and spent hundreds and hundreds of dollars. The vet asked if we wanted to spend some time with Sugar before the euthanasia, so we did. He told us to call him when we were ready.

I held Sugar while the vet gave him the injection. I remember feeling Sugar's heart stop. It was very sad, but it was also a huge relief because Sugar had suffered. I probably prolonged his suffering because I loved him. I did not want to put him to sleep.

When his heart stopped, I knew there was no way I could change my mind. It was done. We stayed with Sugar for about a half hour, and I was not crying anymore. I was relieved that it was over. We held Sugar and petted him. I wrapped a towel around his body, leaving his head out, and then laid him down. The vet said that we could go whenever we wanted. He didn't ask us to pay.

Prior to putting Sugar to sleep, we had decided that we wanted to privately cremate him because what normally happens is that many animals are cremated together. Rarely is a cat privately cremated unless the owner wants to keep his ashes. At the crematory, we were told that his urn and ashes would be ready in two weeks.

On the day we put Sugar to sleep, we did not go home. We went shopping and to lunch. We tried to do everything we could so we would not think of him.

Taking care of him through his illness was much more difficult than being without him. Watching someone you love so
much deteriorate is a horrible experience.

I felt angry because we had put so much effort into saving
Sugar. I couldn't believe it didn't work. I thought that if you
love someone this much and you go to the nth degree to save
him, then there is no way that it can't work. But it didn't.

I do not feel guilty for putting Sugar to sleep because I know
I tried everything humanly possible to save him. I prayed that he
would live and make it through each bout of the illness. He went
through phases. Every time he got better, I would think, Oh,
God, it's working, but I wasn't being realistic. Sugar was too sick.

I'm glad that we privately cremated Sugar and that we are
comfortable having his urn in our bedroom. We don't talk
much about him, but he is here. I feel his spirit is in one of our
other cats named Cream. He is a blonde cream Persian, and he
looks like Sugar except that he is fatter. Even though the two
cats never met, Cream wraps himself around Sugar's urn and
sleeps there. None of our other cats do that.

I needed more support when I was trying to keep Sugar
alive than when I finally made the decision to put him to sleep.
By that time I was at peace with the decision. I felt there was
no other option. My husband was my biggest supporter. My
close friends also went through the experience with me. People
were very supportive by reassuring me that it was normal to
feel the way I felt, and they shared their stories of when they
lost their pets.

When Sugar was sick, I thought about him all the time. I
pulled out of activities in which I was involved. I was sad and
very depressed. I remember that one night when my husband
took me out to dinner, I couldn't even eat my food because I
was crying so much. I couldn't stand the thought of putting
Sugar to sleep.

I learned through this experience that I have a huge capacity to love that I didn't know I had. I am definitely not lazy or

selfish when it comes to investing in or doing what I need to do for an animal.

I also learned that I do not want to have any children because of the pain I experienced with Sugar. To love a child so much and to see the child deteriorate would be more than I could bear. I would be afraid of what might happen if I let the child board a school bus or ride a bike. I could lose that child. I do not want to ever love anyone that much again.

I feel good that I didn't give up on Sugar and that I researched every possible solution. I did not listen to what one vet told me, but I went that extra mile to save Sugar because I loved him so much. I know that I did everything possible to save Sugar.

Lady, Sophie, Bandit, and Ingrid

AS REMEMBERED BY

Laura Hirt, D.V.M.

*"Euthanasia is a good option to have when an animal's illness is fatal.
I don't like to watch an animal waste away and suffer.
Euthanasia is the only humane act at that point."*

When I first started my veterinary practice, I would cry for every animal that I had to euthanize. As a vet, I enjoy working with people and animals, but I also have to be able to euthanize an animal who is wagging her tail and licking my face. Vets have to be strong when putting an animal to sleep. I have the reputation in this area that I won't put any animal to sleep, but personally, I think that euthanasia is a good option to have when an animal's illness is fatal. I don't like to watch an animal waste away and suffer. Euthanasia is the only humane act at that point.

Veterinary medicine is a rewarding profession. I feel good when my staff and I send an animal home. I feel that we did something to help the animal stay alive. I had a case where the pet owner brought her dog into the clinic because the dog had eaten a rag, and the dog was vomiting and having diarrhea. I had the dog on an IV drip for a couple of days, but her condition wasn't getting better, so I decided to do surgery. Some parts of the rag had gotten stuck in her small intestine and stomach, so I had to remove about a foot of the intestine. We kept the dog for five days. When he started eating and drinking, we sent him home. I feel happy when an animal goes home.

Some of the cases that upset and sadden me are the animals who have broken legs that can be fixed but whose pet owners don't have the money. While I understand that some people don't have the money for x-rays, surgery, and follow-up, I become upset when people do have the money but do not want to spend it on their dog. Unfortunately, I see that often. Some people refuse to do what needs to be done, and their animals have to suffer.

Euthanasia is like a double-edged sword. People have difficulty knowing what the right choice should be, but I can't make the choice for them. I have a few clients who refuse to put their pets to sleep because of their own feelings about euthanasia, so they would rather watch their animals die slowly. This is also frustrating because it is difficult to see sick animals go home and continue to suffer.

I am thankful that most of the decisions of putting animals to sleep take place over the telephone because we don't receive enough training in grief counseling in veterinary school. It can be hard to comfort the pet owners who are putting their animal to sleep. Most of the pet owners will cry, and I usually cry along with them. A lot of times, they want to be left alone after their animal has been euthanized. I allow them to have the choice of being with their animal during the process.

The majority of my clients are women because women are the primary caretakers. They are the ones that take the time to bring the animals to the veterinarian's office for their physical checkups. Occasionally, a woman's husband and children will come along, but that is less common. The woman is usually the one who will bring the animal to be put to sleep.

Women are more open with their grief than men when their pets are put to sleep. I have seen women weeping in the office while the men try hard not to cry. In our society, men are not supposed to cry, but I believe that grief is the same for both women and men.

When clients come to put an animal to sleep, they want to know what happens to the pet after it is euthanized. They are concerned because they have heard horror stories about the garbage dump. We try to help them with their concerns and the burial arrangements. We ask them if they want us to take care of the body or if they want to bury their pet. The caretaker at the cemetery will bury the animal or have it cremated. Most of the time he will cremate several animals together because it is less expensive. The cost of an incinerator can be as much as fifteen thousand dollars, so if nobody wants the ashes, it is more economical for him to cremate several animals at one time. If the pet owners want the ashes, cremation is more expensive.

Some people think that veterinary medicine should be less expensive than human medicine because we are working with animals, but we use the same equipment and drugs that are used in human hospitals. My x-ray machine is no different from the x-ray machine that is used in a human hospital. Some veterinarians are using ultrasound machines in animal hospitals, but I have not bought one because they are expensive. The Fremont animal hospital and our hospital cooperate regarding the equipment and special services. If the Fremont animal hospital has a service that I don't have, I send my clients over there. This arrangement works because it is expensive to buy all the equipment. An x-ray machine, for example, can cost about twenty thousand dollars. Veterinary medicine is a major investment.

I have a hard time giving my clients advice on their loss because every individual is different. Some people will do better if they adopt another animal right away because the new pet will keep their mind off the one they lost. They must keep in mind that they are not replacing the animal that died; instead, they are getting a different animal.

I have had wonderful moments with my animals who have died, and I had a strong bond with each one of them. The first time I lost a pet was when I was in junior high school. I was in the second grade when we adopted Lady. We were at a family

reunion, and one of the neighboring farms had a bunch of puppies. The owner gave me a puppy. Lady was about six weeks old
when she came to live with us. When she was two years old,
she was hit by a car, and her right front leg was paralyzed. Later
in life she developed a terrible sore that wouldn't go away, and
she kept licking it. My mother loved animals, but she was not
good about cleaning Lady's ears or treating the sore. Lady
would follow my mom everywhere.

Lady was eleven years old when she was put to sleep. When
I look back, I still cry. I wish that we hadn't done it because I
don't think it was her time. I was old enough to take care of
her, but I was busy with school and other activities. As Lady
grew older, she had difficulty getting up and down because her
leg kept bothering her. She also had a lot of allergies and was incontinent. One day my cousin and I took her to the vet and left
her. I cried when we left. That was hard, and I'm still dealing
with it because I feel that we didn't do the right thing for Lady.

My profession as a veterinarian helps me to cope with the
loss of my own pets because I see death at work, but it is still
different when my pet is involved. I had a little dog named
Sophie who died of liver cancer. I had been working as a vet
for five years, and one of my clients brought in Sophie with a
broken leg. My client didn't have the money to fix it, so I
adopted Sophie and took her home with me. Sophie was a
brave little dog. She went to work with me almost every day.

When Sophie was six and a half years old, she started having
episodes of pain, so I ran blood tests on her. It was her liver. I
did a liver biopsy and discovered that her liver was full of
tumors. I gave her medication whenever she was in pain. I was
selfish because I kept her around for a while. I wasn't ready to
let her go. I felt that as long as she was eating and was walking
around, she was okay. Sophie did all right for a couple of
months, but then she had some episodes where she would fall
over. She lost control of her body. Eventually, I put her to sleep.
I cried for days.

I have quite a few animals buried in my woods, and Sophie is buried there too. I don't have tombstones on their graves, so I don't remember where they are buried. I know they are here with me.

Recently, I lost a couple of my favorite animals. I had a little Pekingese dog, Bandit, whom I loved dearly. She was an older dog when I got her. Bandit came into the clinic because she was urinating all over the house and the owners wanted her to be put to sleep, so I took care of her. She was incontinent because she had a bladder stone, and her owners hadn't taken her to a veterinarian. I removed the bladder stone and put her on antibiotics. Her body grew healthy and strong. I gave her several baths, and her beautiful hair grew back. She was a beautiful and smart dog.

Bandit looked like a little gremlin when she first came into the office. She had these huge eyes, and she had hair only on her face. Her skin was oily, and she had fleas all over her body. Bandit was ugly then, but she had a great personality.

Bandit was a good dog, so I would take her to work with me. We had a strong bond for four years, then she developed a tumor on her ear. I had her tumor taken care of at the Ohio State hospital. Her doctor recommended follow-up radiation. I would have had it done at a human hospital, but none of the hospitals would put an animal on their exam tables. My little dog needed radiation, but I didn't have time to take her to Columbus for her treatments.

A year later the tumor grew back, so I started chemotherapy. Bandit died unexpectedly after the first treatment. I had her at home when she died, and it was awful. I missed her a lot after she died because we had a special bond. Bandit was my dearest pet.

I received a female dog named Ingrid from a friend. Her husband didn't want the dog because they had three male dogs. Ingrid was a great runner, but she would stay close to home. In her later years she developed a cancer that manifested itself with skin lesions. She wasn't eating well, but she would still get into the neighbor's garbage.

I came home one afternoon to let the dogs out, and Ingrid wasn't around. I found her lying in my daughter's room. Ingrid looked at me and didn't even get up. I thought that it was a good day to put her to sleep because she had been uncomfortable for a couple of weeks. When I came home late that night, she came out to greet me and was wagging her tail. I wished that she would lie down and pretend that she wasn't feeling well. I had decided that I was going to put her to sleep because she had a terrible smell. She did nothing but lick her body. Her rectum had swollen, and she was having difficulty with her bowels. She couldn't eat by herself, so I had to help.

Ingrid had deer meat to eat on her last night before I put her to sleep. After she ate, I put her in the bathroom, where the other dogs couldn't come in. We had some special time together with Ingrid, then I put her to sleep. On June 20, 1996, Ingrid passed away at the age of thirteen.

While it was difficult for me when Ingrid died, she had a full life unlike Sophie, who was still young when she died. I am sad when a young animal has to be put to sleep. The older ones have had a chance to be around for a while.

I become upset when people say that I am not doing the right thing by adopting so many animals. If I didn't adopt them, they would be euthanized. I have a full-time job, and I still take good care of them. All my dogs are in the house, and they have blankets on the floor and a couch to sleep on. They have heat and air conditioning, and I make sure they have plenty of food and water.

I built the house around my animals because I love them very much. If tomorrow I won the twenty-million-dollar lottery, I would turn my barn into a giant cat condo, and we would all be happy.

Strawberry and Lady Bird

AS REMEMBERED BY

Elizabeth Wilson

*"What helped me to go through the grief was time and
having good memories and having my parents."*

A friend from church gave me a guinea pig named
Strawberry. Strawberry was reddish with white fur on
her face and between her two ears. I would put her in
my wagon without her cage and take her around the block, and
she wouldn't climb out of the wagon. Strawberry was gentle,
but since I was so little, I wasn't very gentle with her. I carried
her around with me.

Strawberry didn't die, but I had my first experience with pet
loss because I had to leave her behind when we moved to
Saudi Arabia. I felt sad because I didn't want to leave Strawberry. I was angry with Saudi Arabia because I couldn't take my
guinea pig. If we took her, we would be allowed in the country, but she wouldn't. I wasn't angry with my parents because
they couldn't help me. We had to give her away.

On our last day together, I took her to a merry-go-round in
the middle of a courtyard. Riding it was something that I loved
to do, but I had never done it with Strawberry. On the last day
we did it together.

My parents and my sister went with me when I left Strawberry at my friend's house. I waited until the last day to take

Strawberry over. I gave her to my friend, who had a male guinea pig, and took off.

When I was in Saudi Arabia, I would think about Strawberry. One day I figured out that by then any normal guinea pig would have died. I made a little pretend grave and put flowers around it. There is a weed with pinkish white flowers that grows everywhere in Saudi Arabia. I picked the flowers and arranged them in the shape of a rectangle like a grave. I had a funeral for Strawberry as my way of mourning.

I was in the third grade when I received Lady Bird from some people who couldn't keep her. They sold the bird, her cage, and food to my parents for six dollars. She wasn't doing well at the time—the owners thought she was scared. When they wanted to catch Lady Bird, they would chase her into the bathroom and turn off the light. It scared her a lot.

I took Lady Bird and loved her. She and I grew close. She would hide in my hair and peck my ear. Her claws would tickle my neck. Lady Bird had a mirror in her cage that she liked. She would open her mouth and move her beak around. She thought that the reflection was another bird. I loved it when Lady Bird climbed on my hand, and I taught her how to climb on my finger. I tried to train her to say my name, but she never did. She had a soft chest and I would kiss it. I had her for four years.

As I grew older, I became busier and would sometimes ignore Lady Bird. I would even get mad at her, and she became a little afraid of me. After behaving this way, I would think what a terrible person I was. I believed that soon I would have enough time to play with her, but she died before I did. That gave me a lot of guilt, and it took a lot of praying to overcome my guilt.

Toward the end, Lady Bird would squeak with every breath she took. We took her downstairs because we thought that maybe it was too hot upstairs. Then we took her to the groomer's to see if it was her beak. The woman said that Lady

Bird was having problems breathing and that we needed to take her to a vet.

We drove Lady Bird to the vet. Her cage was covered because it was winter. She couldn't see anything, so she was scared. The vet grabbed her without giving her his finger to perch on first. Lady Bird was not used to being grabbed, and she became more scared and died. The vet hurried to the other room to give her some air with a machine, but it was too late. I was scared and sad. I was standing next to my mom, holding her hand. The vet gave us back Lady Bird wrapped in a bag. My mom went to the desk to pay, and the staff told us that we didn't have to pay. Other people were coming into the vet's office to have their pet looked at, and we were going out with our dead bird. I felt funny. I cried all the way home.

We had the funeral that night. My dad helped me by saying a prayer. He talked about Lady Bird. The saddest thing was when we took Lady Bird out of the bag. I put the bag on the frozen ground and pulled it away. Lady Bird rolled out and was all limp and warm. She was warm against all the coldness of winter, and that was heartbreaking for me. I put her in the ground. When we went back inside, I went upstairs to cry. I don't like to cry in front of people. My room felt empty—I felt empty.

My mom felt guilty because she had taken Lady Bird to the vet. She said, "I'm sorry, Elizabeth. If I hadn't taken Lady Bird to the vet, she might still be alive." She said that if I hadn't insisted on going to the groomer's to check on her beak, maybe Lady Bird would still be alive. We all felt guilty wondering what we had done wrong. I thought I was a bad owner. I didn't blame myself for her sickness because she had that squeak for a long time. I felt guilty about how I would get angry at her because she bit me. I understand that it wasn't my mom's fault or the vet's or mine. I wasn't angry at my mom or the vet. She wouldn't have lived much longer.

Most people feel disloyal about getting another pet, but I wanted another pet. I was sad, but I thought it would help to adopt another pet. I wanted another bird so I could give it all the attention that I didn't give Lady Bird. I don't think Lady Bird would have minded. I missed being able to play with Lady Bird when I was done with my homework. It was harder losing Lady Bird than Strawberry because I had her longer.

I went to a funeral for my grandpa after Lady Bird died. I sort of felt the same way as I had with Lady Bird, but I have always felt that humans are more important. The death of a pet is a smaller version of a human death. My grandpa was very sick, and he knew that he was sick. He started to recover, and he was hoping that he would live, but he died. I was angry because I thought that he was okay. Now I believe that my grandpa is in heaven and doesn't need his cane anymore.

God helped me through the grief. I have a strong faith. When I lost Lady Bird, I prayed about it a lot. I don't think I can give advice to other people because I don't know what they are going through. I would comfort them, but I don't think I would give them advice. They have to figure it out on their own. What helped me to go through the grief was time and having good memories and having my parents.

Rocky, Eugene, Pancho, Maybe, and Others

AS REMEMBERED BY

Michael Scott Karpovich, CSP

*"Mourning is not grieving over the fact that a person
has suffered as much as it is mourning the fact that this
person won't be there to meet my needs anymore."*

I grew up on a farm with a lot of animals. My mom, who has been an animal fanatic ever since she was a child, always said that when she had her own home, she would have animals in it. And did she ever: skunks, raccoons, squirrels, dogs, and cats.

The first animal I remember was my "older brother," Rocky, a white German shepherd with a pink nose. My parents had decided to try out pets before they tried out children. Rocky was a very athletic dog. My father had trained him to leap seven-foot fences.

My earliest memories are of my mom, dad, and big brother, Rocky. Rocky was a fun animal. He played and romped and was very protective. He protected me and my other siblings. Most people were scared of him.

We had ducks and when the ducklings were born, Rocky was very excited. He tried to play with them. He would gently grab them in his mouth, throw them up in the air, and accidentally kill them.

Rocky was my father's dog. My parents explained to me, "This is Rocky. He came first." That is how he was introduced to me.

Rocky lived to be thirteen years old. I was twelve when he died. The last year of his life he had cancer. We did various things to keep him alive. Rocky became so miserable that my father had to put him to sleep, which he did by shooting him, and that was so hard on my father. My father is a very tough Ukrainian Cossack who never sheds a tear. When he had to kill his dog, he cried.

I did not hear the shots—my father tried to keep it a secret as to how Rocky died. My father had taken Rocky out and given him a bowl of his favorite food. When my father shot Rocky, Rocky looked up at my father and appeared surprised. That made it all the harder. My father shot him again. It took two or three shots. My father worked hard to clean up Rocky to make him presentable for the funeral. My father was very sensitive about the whole process.

We buried Rocky and had a little funeral. Rocky was laid out on a blanket, and the family gathered around. We each talked a little bit about him before my father buried him. Rocky was more important to the older children than the younger ones.

I also had a pet raccoon named Eugene at the same time we had Rocky. He was another of my older brothers. We used to tease him mercilessly by giving him sugar cubes. Because raccoons wash their food in water before they eat, Eugene would wash his sugar cubes, and they would disappear. He would be so frustrated.

Eugene loved to get into Rocky's mouth. He would stick his snout into Rocky's mouth. He would clean Rocky's teeth. It was the most amazing thing to watch.

Eugene had long nails and was a wild animal, and my parents thought that he was scratching me too much while we played. They took him out to the river and put him on a stone. He was so confused. He went under the water and came back. He did this for hours. Finally, we left him and I felt we had deserted him. It was hard.

We came back a couple days later and called Eugene, and we heard a big splash. A sixty-pound raccoon came swimming to us. We came back a month later and he had grown so huge. Toward the end, he was a wild raccoon. He would come to us and let us throw food to him, but he wouldn't come too close. I felt sad about that. One day we came and yelled, but he didn't appear. I realized that I would never see him again. He had either gone completely wild or had been trapped by a hunter. That was hard for me to accept.

We had a fantasy about what had happened to him. Our fantasy was that he was still out in the river, catching fish and living very independently. Without a corpse, we were sure that Eugene was out there doing crazy things.

The first dog I considered mine was a dachshund named Pancho. I had had cats, but he was my first dog.

Pancho had a unique ability to smile. He would curl up his lips and bare his teeth. Most people thought he was growling. We would tell him, "Smile, Pancho," and he would smile.

Although I felt that Pancho was mine, I think Pancho tried the hardest to impress my father. My father never called him "Pancho." He insisted on calling him "Schultz" after Sergeant Schultz on *Hogan's Heroes*. He was a fat, humongous dog.

Pancho had one passion above everything: he loved to eat. I have pictures of him with his little dachshund hind end sticking out of the garbage can. He would knock over the garbage can and scrounge for food. He was also very amorous. We saw a lot of little Dachshunds running around in our neighborhood, and since the only dachshund in town was Pancho, we had him fixed.

Pancho died because he was so overweight, his back broke. He was about twelve years old when he died. He died a year and a half after Rocky did.

My mother had a dog named Maybe who was a mutt. She was given her name because maybe she was this or maybe she was that. When my grandparents came from Indiana, Maybe came with them. She rode in a huge box strapped in the car.

I vividly remember Maybe's death because it was such a shock to me. I was in the third grade. My grandfather walked me across the road to catch the school bus. Maybe followed us across. A little white Volkswagen came along and hit her. She flew straight up in the air. Being a child, I felt like it was miles in the air. She landed on the other side of the road in a ditch. My school bus arrived at the same moment, and I didn't have time to mourn or cry. I did not have time to say anything. I didn't even have time to see the dog, and that was devastating to me. I climbed on the bus and went to school. I remember staring at the clock and thinking that a few moments ago our dog was killed, and here were all these kids, none of them knowing and none of them caring. It was so weird. I was upset, and I couldn't tell them what had happened.

When I did get home from school, everyone had dealt with the death, and it was over for them. I hadn't had time to process the loss. I talked with my parents, my mom expressed her concern more than my father. I felt I had missed out. The time to mourn was right when Maybe died. And that chance was ripped away from me because I climbed up in the bus and rode away, wanting to cry but not wanting to cry and knowing that Maybe was gone forever. I should have been home crying and I wasn't. That was difficult.

I spent several months thinking about Maybe's death. I felt envious of my grandfather, my grandmother, my mother, and my sister, who were able to be home and deal with it. They had the opportunity to process it, but they weren't even at the scene. My grandfather and I were there. But I didn't get to mourn— I lost my chance. I was part of the death, part of the loss. It was the last experience I shared with Maybe. I would have liked to have been able to sob and cry and touch her. I arrived home and she was in the ground.

The first cat I remember was Merlin, a male Siamese, who could talk. One time he came in the house and jumped onto my grandmother's lap and started making sounds. My grandmother asked, "What's wrong?" She would talk to him, and Merlin would respond. I was very young, but I vividly remember this. I have childhood pictures of Merlin and me. He was a very intelligent cat. He was loving, expressive, and warm.

One day I went outside and called him, and he didn't come. I looked and looked. I found him curled up on top of a fifty-gallon barrel. I went to pat him, and he was stiff. It scared me. I couldn't believe it. His death was such a loss. I was just beginning to comprehend that creatures die, and I was devastated. There wasn't anything wrong with him, and I didn't know why he had to die. He was my buddy.

Some of the most painful losses were the losses of Mr. Hahn, a white cat with one blue eye and one green eye, and O.J., an orange cat who slept on the roof. I named Mr. Hahn after my teacher. These cats just disappeared one day like Eugene. They were not on the road. They weren't in the ditch. I called them but couldn't find them. I looked for their bodies but couldn't find them. These are the most disturbing types of loss because I feel stuck in the grieving process. What could have happened to them? Sometimes I wish I could find something tangible so I could say, "There it is. That is what happened to Mr. Hahn." I want that closure.

While I was in college, we had a little kitten named Samantha who was the runt of the litter. Samantha was a tiny kitten. She had a whisper of a meow that was barely audible. She was four to five inches long while the others in the liter were a foot long.

Samantha loved to sleep with me in bed. One time she curled up next to my back, and when I rolled onto my back, I accidentally killed her. I could not forgive myself. I kept asking why I didn't feel her. It hurt me, and I still feel vulnerable when I tell others about it.

Some people when they found out about it made jokes and laughed. Their attitude enraged me. Her death was such a loss, and I felt completely responsible for it. I adored this little thing. I loved small things and collected miniatures. And here was this tiny kitten, curling up into my back, loving me with her little heart, and I killed her.

This was another time when my father showed his true self and sensitivity. When he came in to wake me up, he knew what had happened. He was very sensitive to my feelings. I buried her alone. I couldn't do it with my family. I was so ashamed, so torn up, and I didn't want anyone to know. It was a very difficult loss, and I still feel incredibly guilty.

Living on a farm has helped me cope with death. I've become good at mourning and at accepting loss. I've held a lot of funerals for significant animals. Even when a sheep or a cow died, there was a semblance of a funeral. We would dig a hole and bury it. There was still a sense of farewell.

If Rocky had been the only pet that had died, I would not have learned much. My losses had to include all of our pets—Rocky, Pancho, Merlin, Eugene, Maybe, and Samantha—before I could realize the reality of the circle of life. There comes a time to harvest and there comes a time to plant. I realize that they were a part of me, and in some way they will always be there.

Going through the stages of grieving with Rocky, Pancho, and Eugene helped prepare me for losing my grandfather and my grandmother. It was like practice. I could handle the grieving process and the loss better because I knew what it was like. In the end, mourning is not grieving over the fact that a person has suffered as much as it is mourning the fact that this person won't be there to meet my needs anymore. When grandmother and grandfather died, I cried, not because they had suffered but because I had lost them. When Rocky and Pancho died, I cried because they were not going to be there to be my companions anymore.

My family sometimes debated whether there was an animal heaven or not. My mother would assure me there was a heaven by saying, "God promises that when we get to heaven, we will be happy, and can you imagine being happy without Pancho, without Rocky?" And at the moment I couldn't.

I wasn't good at making friends with people, but I was good at making animal friends. People are so frustrating; animals are so straightforward. You have to realize that cats are selfish and may think that you are their pet. Dogs are the ultimate givers. Most dogs will do whatever it takes to get you to say, "Okay, I forgive you and I love you again."

Fair Molly MCQ

AS REMEMBERED BY

Judy Neely

"I was thinking of Molly and feeling bad, so I drove to a place where I used to take her. Over the area was a rainbow. I cried."

I first saw Molly, a Boston terrier, in a pet shop in Missoula, Montana. Molly was in a cage, and she had the biggest eyes that I have ever seen. I fell in love with her eyes, which were full of love and joy. I put my fingers through the cage and let her lick them. She jumped up and down, then she sat and looked at me.

I decided to buy Molly. I bought the supplies I needed for her, then picked her up as I went out the door. I held her in the air and told her that she looked like a guppy. She was only eight weeks old. She was a little dog with a short screw tail.

I drove home to Hamilton, where I lived in a mobile home nestled up against the Bitterroot Mountains. Molly slept most of the way home. When we arrived home, I was scared to set her down because I had a lot of wilderness on my property. When I did set her down, she ran fifty laps around my mobile home. Molly was going as fast as she could go. I chased her through the trees and around the trailer before I finally caught her.

When I took her into the house, Dino, my four-month-old Doberman pinscher, was sitting on the floor. I told him that I had a friend for him and put Molly on the floor. Dino took one look at her, and he ran ninety miles an hour down the hall and into my bedroom. Molly ran after him, and I followed her. When I was about halfway down the hall, Dino was coming back full speed the other way. He ran between my legs, causing me to lose my balance and sending me crashing to the floor. Molly landed on top of me.

Since it was a hot day, I took both dogs down to the Bitterroot River for a swim. I put Dino in the back of the truck, and Molly sat up front with me. When we got to the river, Dino ran into the water and swam. Molly was so tiny that I was afraid she would fall in. She walked to the edge of the water as if she wanted to swim, but I stopped her. Dino and Molly played together at the river, and by the time we arrived back home, they had become friends.

Molly was a tough and courageous dog. If she thought Dino was going to get in trouble, she would sit between his front legs and look at me with an expression that said, "I dare you to yell at him or get him in trouble." Molly was afraid of thunder, though, so she would sit next to Dino whenever there was a storm.

We lost Dino in July 1992 when he was only five years old. He was hit by a car while at my folks' house. I was upset and sad. Molly missed her playful buddy. She would trot up and down the hall of the mobile home looking for him.

Our trips to McDonald's and Baskin Robbins started when Molly was very young. When I reached the drive-up window, Molly would climb on my lap with her two front paws on the truck window and her head sticking out. The cashier would give Molly a box of McDonald's cookies, and she would put them on the seat. Then she would come back and get the bag with our hamburger and French fries. I would usually order a double burger and give Molly one of the patties. Molly would eat the hamburger patty, and then she would help me eat the French fries.

Molly loved all kinds of ice cream. She would get her own ice-cream cone whenever we went to Baskin Robbins. Sometimes she would have yogurt because I didn't want her to get too fat. If I would get my ice cream in a cup, she would eat off a spoon. When I was getting ready to go somewhere with Molly, I would leave the truck door open on purpose and pretend to be looking for her. She would sneak into the truck and fake sleeping. She loved the truck; it was her haven.

Molly and I never had to talk. I could look at her face and know what she was thinking. She also seemed to know what I was thinking. If I was crying or felt bad, she would look at me with her big eyes as if to say, What's wrong? I would tell her that I loved her, and she would look at me like she was saying, You know, Mom, I love you too. She was so expressive.

Molly gave a lot of love to people. I was a director of an Alzheimer's care unit in Missoula, and Molly would go to work with me every day. We had patients who couldn't communicate or talk to the staff, but they would talk to Molly. She would play with the patients during their activity time. Molly would stay on the beds of the dying and would comfort patients and their families.

Her favorite pastime was cleaning up the floor after lunch. Sometimes the patients would set their plates of food on the floor for her. Molly was delighted, but the staff was horrified and would come to the patients' "rescue."

Molly was my best friend and my child. I would have never put her in a position where she could get hurt or lost. I would have given my life for her.

On March 14, 1995, she had a grand mal seizure. I was devastated. The seizure scared me so much that I called her vet, Dr. Pruyn. He said that the seizures would come in clusters and if she continued to have them, we would start her on medication. I bargained with God. I prayed that he would let her live another year. She lived another fifteen months after the first seizure.

She grew worse in June 1996. She had difficulty sleeping. She wasn't able to lie down because she couldn't breathe, so she had to sleep sitting up. When Dr. Pruyn tested her air capacity, he found she was not obtaining enough oxygen. He told me that it was time to consider putting Molly to sleep.

I couldn't talk to Molly about putting her to sleep. Carol, my friend, said that I needed to give Molly permission to die. She said that Molly was only getting up in the morning because of me, so I had to tell Molly that she could go.

I took Molly to the backyard and told her that she could go. If she needed to leave, it was okay with me. I told her how much I loved her. I kissed her. After I gave her permission, she seemed to grow a little worse. I took her back to the vet and told him about a medication I had heard of that is given to people who have fluid in their stomachs. He gave it to her, and the next day she was much better. I took her for a ride in the truck. She was bright eyed.

Two days later, she was again having a hard time breathing. I sat on the steps and read Molly poems. She sat next to me and never took her eyes off of me. She reached up and licked my face.

The next morning, I took her into Dr. Pruyn. Her oxygen level was low. Dr. Pruyn said that it was time to let her go.

I left the clinic and took Molly to see a priest. He sat on the floor and read her a story, "The Blessing of the Animals," and made the sign of the cross on her forehead. Then I took Molly to McDonald's. I bought her French fries, but she couldn't eat them. We went to Baskin Robbins, and she ate some yogurt, and then I took her home for a while.

When I returned to the clinic, Dr. Pruyn told me that he was willing to do the euthanasia at my house. I decided to have Molly euthanized in her haven, our truck. The truck was her life. We were always on the road. We lived in the truck more than we lived in the house.

I climbed into the truck and Molly lay on my lap. I played the song "Good Night, My Angel" by Billy Joel. I held her, loved her, and kissed her. She was lying on my lap when Dr. Pruyn put her to sleep. In no more than a second, she was relaxed and gone. Dr. Pruyn and his assistant left me with Molly for a while. Carol, who had come to support me, held Molly, then I held her.

After the euthanasia, I told Dr. Pruyn that I was having a terrible time coping because Molly trusted me. Putting her to sleep was the hardest thing that I had ever done in my life. He reassured me that I had done what was right for Molly—I had given her one last gift. Molly would have died a terrible death if she had not been put to sleep. She could have choked to death. This way she went with the dignity she deserved.

The first night after the euthanasia, I was numb. The next day I felt like somebody was turning a knife in my heart. I felt that life did not have a purpose. Life was dull without Molly.

I don't have the same happiness and peace in my life that I had when Molly was alive. I have never been so unhappy. I take care of the needs of my other dogs, but I am unable to give myself to them. When I see other people with their dogs, I don't want to look at them. I don't want to watch their relationships because I'm hurting so bad inside.

I could never be angry at Molly because I know that she would never have left me if she didn't have to. I wasn't mad at God, but I was heartbroken. I can't be angry at God because he gave her to me, and I always knew that someday he would take her back. But handing her back to God was the hardest thing I have ever done in my life. A part of me died with Molly.

I felt a lot of guilt. I felt that if I had done things differently, Molly would still be here. I felt that I shouldn't have taken her life so early. I wish that I could change things so that Molly was still here with me. I wait for the day when God comes for me. I look for help from heaven. I want God and the angels to watch over Molly.

I wanted to have a memorial service for Molly, but I couldn't because I was so heartbroken. I had a special urn made for her. The urn is a statue of a Boston terrier that was sculptured to look like Molly. The urn has a wooden base with her name and dates on it. I keep fresh flowers by the urn, and every Monday night at ten o'clock, I burn a candle for the Rainbow Bridge and for all the dogs in the world. I always kiss Molly good night.

I kept her toys and beanbag—they are exactly where she left them. I also kept her shirts, coats, and blanket. Her food dish is still in the same spot too.

I find myself talking to Molly constantly, and I write letters to her. I have written poems about her. I know that she is gone, but I keep hoping that she is still at my side. Molly is in my heart and mind.

Every day I look for signs of reassurance. A friend of mine sent me a card that read, "Butterflies are the reflection of God's love, and Molly was love." Shortly after that, I saw a butterfly that followed me up a hill and down the other side. I thought it was odd and kept wondering what God was trying to tell me. A week later, I was walking up the hill again and talking to God. I asked him to reassure me that Molly was okay and that I would see her again. A butterfly flew right in front of me. I stopped and watched it fly away. I asked God to send the butterfly back if Molly was okay. I kept walking, and a butterfly appeared in front of my nose. I looked to my right and there was another butterfly. I looked to my left, and there was another butterfly. I was surrounded by at least eight butterflies.

One week after Molly died, I was reading the story "The Rainbow Bridge" and I was skeptical. This is a story someone made up to help people feel better, but there was no evidence that such a place exists. I looked at Molly's beanbag, and over the beanbag was the biggest and brightest rainbow that I had ever seen. I felt Molly was saying, I'm okay. I am here and you will see me again. I felt God was saying, Judy, I have Molly. I promise you that she is all right.

A couple of weeks later on my way to church, I was thinking of Molly and feeling bad, so I drove to a place where I used to take her. Over the area was a rainbow. I cried.

I have not grieved as hard over the death of a human friend as I have for Molly. I didn't know whether to hug Molly or to slap her for causing me this pain. Yet she gave me more love than I could handle in one lifetime. I will never love another animal like I loved Molly. I can't wait to look in her eyes again and to hold her.

What is helping me to cope with Molly's death is being able to share her life with other people. I want them to know about and always remember Molly. She had unconditional love to share with everybody. Molly was very special and she touched so many people with her life.

Molly's death has given me a deep understanding of grief. When people talk to me about their pain, I truly understand how they feel. I learned that the animal-and-human relationship is a bond that is vividly powerful. I also learned that some people do not understand what it is to grieve for a pet, and they can say hurtful things like "Just get another dog."

My advice to anyone who is grieving over the death of a pet is to find someone special to talk to—someone who will understand and stick by your side. You need a person who won't rush you through the grief and tell you to get over it, a person who won't be upset because you are still talking about it four months later, a person who you can cry with and who will give you a hug when you need it.

I don't believe that I will ever speak about Molly without crying. Molly is worth every tear. I may be able to go on with my life, but I never will forget her. I can close my eyes and describe everything about her from the tip of her nose to the tip of her tail. I can describe the smell of her feet, the look in her eyes, and the little spots on her belly.

Molly is a once-in-a-lifetime friend—her soul looked into my soul. Our spirits are attuned to each other. She is my connection with eternity and infinity. I would have given my life for her. If our relationship was a little taste of heaven, then I can't wait until I get to heaven.

Nick

AS REMEMBERED BY

Peter Poses, Ph.D.

"Telling the stories of our losses helps us through the grief. . . . A loss cannot be grieved for if there's no witness, no listener. . . . When the story is told, then we can close the book and it's over."

In our support group are four therapists who act as facilitators. We each take three months of the year, and we rotate with the seasons. I don't introduce myself as a pet loss counselor; I introduce myself as a marriage and family therapist. I became involved in bereavement counseling because I'm interested in the human-and-animal bond, and I have been rewarded with my own personal relationships with dogs. I also started the support group because such support wasn't available for me when I was suffering through the grief of losing my dog, Nick.

I think everybody has his own idea about how much counseling is enough. The biggest struggle for the pet owner is to say goodbye.

I believe that telling the stories of our losses helps us through the grief. Whenever somebody tells his story, he feels better. I believe that a loss cannot be grieved for if there's no witness, no listener. People should be able to share their stories and put their grief and their feelings into words. When the story is told, then we can close the book and it's over—that's the end.

The first dog that I had as an adult was Nick. He died in 1974, which was over twenty years ago. Nick was a family member. He was like a sibling. The cause of his death was unknown. He was running in a park in Boston and that night he had grand mal convulsions. A couple of hours later he died.

In our society, men are brought up to be soldiers—we should hide our feelings. I was beside myself when Nick died, and I cried. I was also depressed. I created a ritual with songs and music. Friends came over, and I shared my stories about Nick. My friends and family were supportive.

Rituals are an important part of grieving. My notion of a ritual or a memorial is creating a context in which one's feelings can be normalized, legitimized, heard, and witnessed. After Nick's death I took ten years before I opened up to Shadow, my other pet. The only memento I have of Nick is a photograph which is sufficient for me.

I strongly believe that part of the grieving process is releasing the anger. I had a lot of anger after Nick died. I was angry that he left me.

The importance of going through grief is that it creates what I call "a resented gift." Everybody resents the pain, but the gift teaches us to access aspects of our humanity. This period is a time to grow, mature, and become more responsible and compassionate. Nick's death taught me that I wasn't as grown up as I had hoped or wished.

I normally don't dream in color, but on the morning after Nick died, I dreamed of him running along green fields and swimming in blue lakes. I felt that my dream signified that I wasn't ready to let him go—I needed to keep him alive in my dream of vivid colors. Nick was so colorful in the dream. The dream brought me a couple of more hours with him.

I feel that the support group helps to make the grief easier for others. The majority of the people who come to the support group are referred by their vets. They are people like myself who have experienced the deaths of their pets. There are more women than men in the group. We make our way around the circle and open up the discussion to whatever stories may arise. I want them to feel safe. They will not be judged, criticized, or made fun of. Sometimes I share my personal story about Nick.

These groups fall into what I would call the psychoeducational area as compared to the therapeutic area. We teach about the stages of grief. A lot of time is spent teaching about the expression of feelings and about the grief process. At the same time, we create some therapeutic moments because it is a support group. I have boxes of tissues on extra chairs when I have my circle. The tissues give people permission to cry. If they are feeling sad and feeling tearful, it's okay because the circle is a safe place to share their tears. We support each other. The group creates its own resourcefulness as far as being there for one another. In essence, every group member becomes a cotherapist—not in a technical way but in a resourceful way.

The challenge is to create a story-telling setting. When anybody tells his story, he feels more at peace, even if it's a horrific and painful story. The purpose is telling the stories and having at least one other person listening.

I hear lots of stories from people who are very anxious because they feel they have grieved more over the death of a pet than they did over a human being such as a parent, grandparent, or sibling. I tell them that it is probably a function of the fact that human relationships are much more complicated. Our relationships with humans are ambivalent. They are always love–hate relationships. With pets our relationships are usually only loving, and that makes the grieving harder.

When it comes to deciding when to get another pet, I tell people that until they are clear that they've told their story and feel finished, they are not ready to say hello and start a new story with a new animal. I want them to make sure it's not going to be a replacement. Each bond should be unique and remarkable in itself. It should not be a throwback to some previous bond that has been lost.

Grief Support Writing

How to Write and Share Your Story of Pet Loss

Harley King

The Power of Writing to Heal the Pain

One of the best salves for healing the pain and grief that you feel is writing. The process of putting your feelings, thoughts, and experiences down on paper will give you the opportunity to work through your pain and sorrow.

Unfortunately, some of you don't feel you can write. You feel that writing is something for professionals with creative talents but not for you. Yet writing is one of the most powerful techniques you have for clarifying your feelings and working through your emotions. By opening yourself up and expressing your pain and grief on paper, you will release the emotions that are suffocating and depressing you. Giving vent to your anger and pain through writing will set you free.

Fifteen Guidelines for Grief Support Writing

I want to share with you a process, that if you follow it, will begin to heal your wounds and help you to recover from your grief:

1. First, read two or three stories from our book.
2. Then write for fifteen minutes every day. Discipline yourself to write even on those days you don't feel like writing. You can use the journal at the end of this book.
3. Write in longhand with a pen or pencil. Do not use a computer.
4. Begin either with the phrase "I remember" or "I feel."
5. Write about the good times you had together with your pet. Write about the bad times. Write about the death.
6. Write without stopping for the full fifteen minutes. Keep your hand moving at all times.
7. Whenever you run out of things to say, begin again with the phrase "I remember" and keep writing.
8. Write without thinking. Give free rein to your emotions and feelings.
9. Feel free to say whatever you want. Don't worry about what others will think.
10. Be as specific as possible in your writing. Put in descriptive detail.
11. Don't try to be creative or cute.
12. Don't worry about spelling or grammar or what your English teacher taught you. You are not writing for a grade.
13. It is okay to cry while you are writing. Keep writing through the tears. Don't stop.
14. Keep writing as long as you need. If you wish, you can expand your writing time to thirty minutes or an hour.
15. Do not share your initial writing with others. They may not understand your expression of your pain or may be hurt by what you write.

Writing and Sharing Your Story

Once you have begun to heal your grief through Grief Support Writing, you may want to turn your experience into a story that will help others heal their pain and give them needed support.

Using the techniques of Grief Support Writing, write out a response to each of the following questions. Be sure to be specific and concrete with the details of your story. Put in details that will help others to picture the story.

After you have written a response to each question, edit your material into a chronological story. Put the story away for three or four days, then rewrite the story as many times as needed to make it read well. Reading the story aloud will help you determine if it sounds good.

Once you are satisfied that you have written it to the best of your ability, submit it for publication or publish it yourself and give to family and friends.

Questions to Help You Write Your Story

1. Identify your pet's name, type of animal, breed, and sex.
2. Describe how you acquired your pet. Was your pet a gift? Adopted? Purchased? Found? What were your thoughts and feelings? Why did you pick his or her name?
3. Describe four to six special moments that you and your pet experienced together.
4. Describe the kind of relationship you and your pet had. Was he or she a friend, a soul mate, a member of the family, or just a pet?
5. Identify the lessons your pet taught you about life.
6. Describe how your pet died. When did your pet die (month/day/year)? How old was your pet when he or she died?
7. If you had your pet euthanized, describe the experience. How did you make the decision? Did you stay with your pet when he or she was put to sleep? How do you feel about euthanasia? Did you feel guilty?
8. Describe your emotions or feelings when you lost your pet. Did you find yourself in shock and unable to believe that your pet was gone? Did you ever feel like withdrawing and hiding from everybody? Did you experience any anger at

yourself? Your pet? Your family and friends? How did you express this anger? Did you try to strike a bargain with God or others to allow your pet to live? Did you feel guilty? Has the sadness ever been overwhelming or paralyzing? Have you ever felt that you have accepted the death of your pet?

9. Describe funeral or burial arrangements. Were there any prayers? Any rituals? Ceremonies? Did you choose burial or cremation? Why?

10. Describe what you did with your pet's special toys, dishes, and leashes. Did you keep them? Give them away? Bury them with your pet? What have you done with the photographs of your pet?

11. If you had other animals around your house when your pet died, describe how they reacted? Did they seem to notice that the pet was gone? What expressions of grief did they display?

12. Describe how you coped with your grief and pain. What helped you to work through the pain and grief? What type of support did you receive from your family and friends? Did you join a support group? Did you grieve by yourself? Did you share your grief with others? Did you seek grief counseling? What has helped you overcome the pain?

13. Describe other experiences that you have had with pet loss. How have you coped with the losses? What have you learned from the different losses? What do you remember about the first pet loss that you experienced?

14. If you ever experienced the death of a relative or close friend, describe the loss. What are the differences between the experience of grieving for a human being and grieving for a pet? What are the similarities?

15. Identify what you learned from the experience of pet loss. Did you learn something about yourself? Did you discover that you were stronger than you thought? Did you discover that you were not as strong as you thought?

16. What advice would you give to someone who was grieving for his or her pet?

Hello Friend

A Journal of
Loving Memories

∽

You will never be forgotten . . .

You will always be in my heart . . .

I love you.

My Loving Friend

Date of Journey to Rainbow Bridge

My Friend

_____
Name

_____
Nickname

_____
Birth Date

_____
Breed

_____
Sex

_____
Color

_____
Eye Color

_____
Mother's Name

_____
Father's Name

_____
Favorite Treat

_____
Favorite Toy

_____
Veterinarian

_"When death ends a relationship,
the feeling of loss is like a
puzzle that is missing a piece."_

MARIA LUZ QUINTANA

"The empty leash hangs on the wall . . . fond memories . . ."

BARBARA BAYNE

"The relationships we share
with loved ones are very
important threads in the
fabric of our existence."

MARIA LUZ QUINTANA

"I may hurt again someday,
but it is worth it."

LORI DESROCHERS

_____

_____

_____

_____

_____

_____

_____   *"I will always cherish my*
                                          best friend and will
_____   *treasure his memory."*

                                          ROSE L. ALLEN

_____

_____

_____

_____

_____

_____

_____

_____

_____

"If our relationship was a little taste of heaven, then I can't wait until I get to heaven."

JUDY NEELY

_____

_____

_____

_____

_____

_____

_____

_____

*"But they will be remembered
with a smile and a tear."*

VIVIAN FELTZ

_____

_____

_____

_____

_____

_____

_____

_____

_____

About the Authors

Maria Luz Quintana

Maria graduated from Bowling Green State University with a degree in ethnic studies. Her inspiration for this book came from a class in death and dying. She realized that there was plenty of research and information about the grieving process that people experience when a human being dies, but very little support was available for people who had lost a favorite pet. Through this book, Maria wants to give people who have lost a pet a voice for their grieving.

Maria lives in Perrrysburg, Ohio, with her husband, Harley. They have one daughter, Johari. Maria has twelve years of experience teaching in preschools. *It's Okay to Cry* is her first book.

Shari L. Veleba

Shari graduated from Bowling Green State University with a degree in Journalism. Shari has experienced pet loss several times over the years. Her most recent loss, a collie named Buppy, led her to consider the relationship between pet loss and human loss. Shari is in communications and lives in Columbus, Ohio. *It's Okay to Cry* is her first book.

Harley King

Harley graduated from Goshen College with a degree in English. For over twenty years, Harley has been writing poetry, fiction, magazine articles, newsletters, training manuals, policy and procedure manuals, ads, and speeches.

Harley has published four previous books: *Winter Silence* (1977), *Empty Playground* (1980), *Mother, Don't Lock Me in That Closet* (1989), and *The World of Speaking* (1995).

Harley has ten years' experience speaking and conducting seminars. He speaks in the areas of leadership, customer service, service recovery, marketing, sales, writing, and pet loss.

Harley lives with his wife, Maria, in Perrysburg, Ohio. They have one daughter, Johari.

Do you want another copy of this book to give to a friend?
Call 1-800-247-6553 to order another copy of this book.

For more information, write to:
K & K Communications
875 Maple Street
Perrysburg, OH 43551

Or E-mail:
HGKing@aol.com
MLQKing@aol.com

*"Over time our tears will help heal the pain
and soothe the hurt."*

HARLEY KING